HEALTH AT YOUR FINGERTIPS

A TREATISE ON MUDRA THERAPY (A BRANCH OF AYURVEDA)

by

Dr. Dhiren Gala

B.Sc., D.H.M.S., D.O., D.Ac., C.G.O., C.C.H., A.R.S.H.

Recipient of a gold medal for extraordinary work in the field of Alternative Therapeutics

With

Dr. D. R. Gala

N.D., D.N.O., D.C.O.

Dr. Sanjay Gala

M.B. (BOM.), M.S. (ENT)

NAVNEET®

NAVNEET PUBLICATIONS (INDIA) LIMITED

G 4555

Visit us at : www.navneet.com | e-mail : npil@navneet.com

Price : Rs. 35.00

Dr. Dhiren Gala
1st Floor, Abbas Building 'A',
Near Tilak Market, Jalbhai Lane,
Harkishandas Hospital Road, Mumbai – 400 004.
Phone : 2386 7275

[1 – 9 – 2007 (4) : 3]

NAVNEET PUBLICATIONS (INDIA) LIMITED

Mumbai : 1. Bhavani Shankar Road, Dadar, **Mumbai – 400 028.** (Tel. 6662 6565 • Fax : 6662 6470)
2. **Navyug Distributors :** Road No. 8, M. I. D. C., Next to Indian Institute of Packaging, Marol, Andheri (East), **Mumbai – 400 093.** (Tel. 2821 4186 • Fax : 2835 2758)

Ahmadabad : Navneet House, Gurukul Road, Memnagar, **Ahmadabad – 380 052.** (Tel. 6630 5000)

Bengalooru : Sri Balaji's, No. 12, 2nd Floor, 3rd Cross, Malleswaram, **Bengalooru – 560 003.** (Tel. 2346 5740)

Chennai : 30, Sriram Nagar, North Street, Alwarpet, **Chennai – 600 018.** (Tel. 2434 6404)

Delhi : 2-E/23, Orion Plaza, 2nd & 3rd Floor, Jhandewalan Extn., **New Delhi – 110 055.** (Tel. 2361 0170)

Hyderabad : Kalki Plaza, Plot No. 67, Krishnapuri Colony, West Maredpalley, **Secunderabad – 500 026.** (Tel. 2780 0146)

Kolkata : 1st Floor, 7, Suren Tagore Road, **Kolkata – 700 019.** (Tel. 2460 4178)

Nagpur : 63, Opp. Shivaji Science College, Congress Nagar, **Nagpur – 440 012.** (Tel. 242 1522)

Nashik : Dharmaraj Plaza, Old Gangapur Naka, Gangapur Road, **Nashik – 422 005.** (Tel. 231 0627)

Navsari : 3/C, Arvind Nagar Society, Lunsikui Road, **Navsari – 396 445.** (Tel. 244 186)

Patna : 1st Floor, 36-D, Sahdeo Mahto Marg, Srikrishnapuri, **Patna – 800 001.** (Tel. 254 0321)

Pune : Navneet Bhavan, 1302, Shukrawar Peth, Near Sanas Plaza, Bajirao Road, **Pune – 411 002.** (Tel. 2443 1007)

Surat : 1, Ground Floor, Sri Vallabh Complex, Kotwal Street, Nanpara, **Surat – 395 001.** (Tel. 246 3927)

Vadodara : F-1, Vaidya Vatika, Opp. Hanuman Wadi, Sardar Bhuvan Khancho, **Vadodara – 390 001.**

CONTENTS

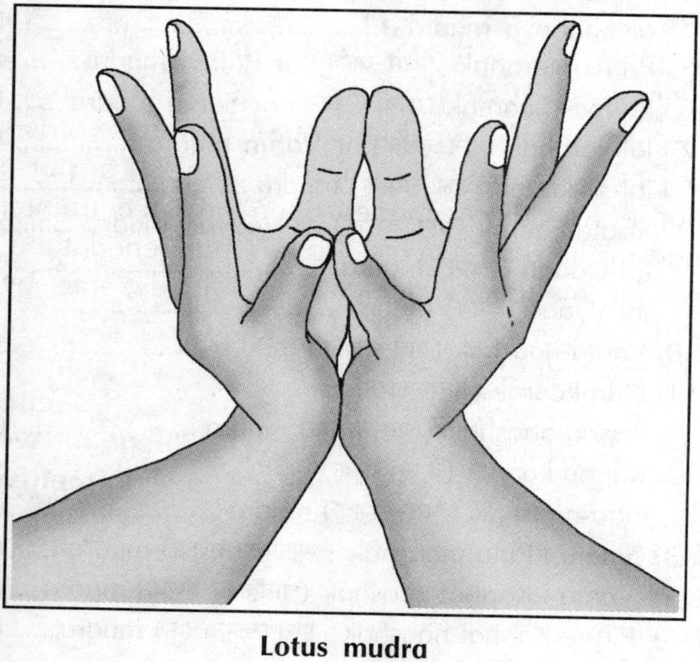

Lotus mudra

SECTION I

1. INTRODUCTION

Medicines are, indeed, a boon to mankind! At times, medicines even save lives. Diseases once believed to be incurable (e.g., tuberculosis) have been completely tamed by medicines and rendered as docile as the proverbial cow. Effective vaccines have eradicated many viral diseases (e.g., small pox) from the surface of the earth.

However, some drawbacks or disadvantages are associated with medicines and medical treatments :

(1) At times medicines only mask symptoms or merely relieve distress, rather than striking at the root causes of illness. Many doctors are inwardly aware of the fact (though they may not admit it openly) that symptoms represent, not a disease but our immunity and, therefore, should never be suppressed.

(2) Medicines are like double-edged swords; they can help but they can harm as well. To put it in popular parlance, medicines often produce unintended or undesirable 'side-effects'. It has happened time and again that medicines declared absolutely safe by the pharmaceutical industry, on the basis of the much-boasted 'double-blind clinical trials', were later found to produce very serious side-effects. Let us cite the example of Thalidomide. Hundreds of pregnant women who took this supposedly harmless sleeping pill gave birth to babies with malformed (seal) limbs. Dr. Dale Friend, the head of the pharmacology department of the renowned Britham Hospital in Boston, Mass., USA, says unequivocally, 'there is nothing like a safe medicine'.

(3) Modern medicines are too powerful weapons to be used against trivial diseases; it is like using a cannon-ball to kill a fly !

(4) After the advent of specialist/super-specialist doctors, five-star hospitals and sophisticated, hi-tech diagnostic instruments, medical treatment has become prohibitively expensive; only the most affluent can easily afford it. God save the poor or the middle-class man who falls ill. All of us have seen families brought to ruin by enormous medical expenses.

(5) Because of the 'not-so-stringent' laws and inefficient (in effect, non-existent) judicial systems, most developing countries are witnessing the appalling problem of adulterated or fake medicines. When buying/ receiving a medicine, many a time we wonder whether the capsules contain the 'real thing' or merely saw-dust !

(6) It, almost always, happens that our body and/ or the germs soon get accustomed or resistant to a particular medicine. When the era of antibiotics dawned with the invention of penicillin by Alexander Fleming, it was believed that all infectious diseases will soon be eradicated from the surface of the earth. That dream, however, has been reduced to shambles. The stark truth is that disease-causing germs soon learn to digest antibiotic toxins. Malarial parasites are, no longer responding to the once infallible chloroquin and malaria is making a spirited comeback throughout the world.

There are two more issues that need further elucidation. Firstly, there are diseases for which satisfactory medical solutions have not yet been discovered. Secondly, there are diseases like diabetes, high blood pressure, etc., which can only be controlled but not cured. Such diseases call for life-long treatment to prevent further deterioration of health and sustain life. Considering the possibilities of adverse side-effects, few people suffering from such diseases would relish the idea of taking medicines throughout life.

Any rational person, who carefully considers these drawbacks of medicines, would have no hesitation in admitting that it would be more logical to tackle diseases through non-medical measures. *But is it possible ? Can diseases be actually 'cured' without resorting to medicines ?* In reply, we will say that there are, indeed, effective non-medicinal therapeutic measures (like Acupuncture, Acupressure*, Naturopathy*, Magnet Therapy*, Reiki Therapy*, etc.) that can be employed to fight diseases. The history of healing is much older than the history of medicine ! We sincerely believe that people should be informed about, and trained in, a few non-medicinal yet effective modes of treatment so that they can treat the 'not so serious' common ailments on their own, at home. Of course, if such non-medicinal 'first line of treatment' proves inadequate, a competent physician should certainly be consulted.

Mudra Therapy is another such non-medical mode of treatment which helps without harming. Mudras (more precisely 'Hasta-mudras') are various postures of fingers and thumbs. In Mudra Therapy, different diseases are treated by holding and retaining the fingers and the thumbs in different ways (see figures on page 8).

---

* Books on these subjects, written by Dr Dhiren Gala and published by Navneet Publications (India) Ltd. are available at all bookshops.

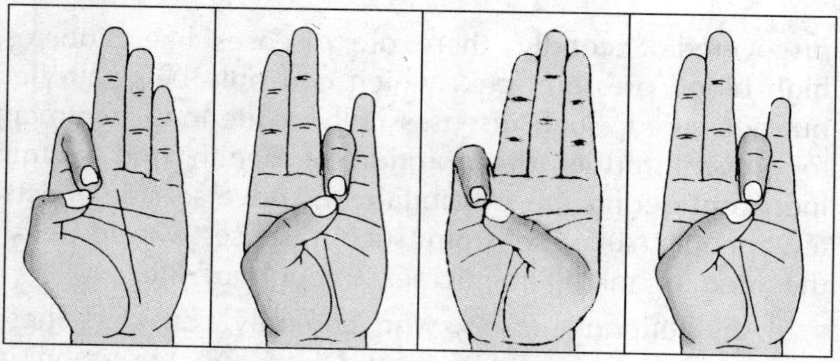

Fig. 1.1

This simple measure surprisingly restores a state of balance (homoeostasis) within the body and raises the level of the performer's resistance. With the patient's immunity thus strengthened, the disease has no other option but to flee.

Mudra Therapy is advantageous in a number of ways :

(1) It is very simple, perhaps the simplest among different non-medical therapies.

(2) Mudras are quite easy to perform. Barring a few people who have stiff/arthritic fingers, most others can practise them without any difficulty.

(3) It is an extremely gentle form of treatment. Therefore, at times, the patient's recovery from illness might seem somewhat slow. However, its efficacy is beyond doubt. Remember : slow and steady wins the race !

(4) It is entirely safe since no chemical medicines are employed.

(5) Mudra Therapy is inexpensive (in fact, free) because no gadgets or instruments are required.

(6) It is a form of self-treatment. Any person who has acquired basic knowledge about mudras can treat

most trivial ailments on his own. As far as medical therapies are concerned, the patient is reduced to a mute spectator in the process of treatment; in Mudra Therapy he is promoted to the role of an active participant !

(7) Mudra Therapy has a preventive aspect, too. Any person who analyses and understands his temperament and his bodily constitution (on the basis of a table given in the next chapter) can realize what ailments he is susceptible to and can, then, regularly practise certain mudras to prevent those susceptibilities from manifesting into overt illnesses. For example, a person having a mercurial temperament or 'Vaata' constitution can perform Vaayu-shaamak or Vaata-naashak mudra for a few minutes every day to avert illness and maintain peak health.

(8) Mudras enjoy a universal application. They can help all types of disorders : sub-acute, acute or chronic; they can help all types of people : young or old, men or women.

(9) Mudra Therapy can be advantageously combined with other forms of treatment : non-medical as well as medical. Being a part of Ayurveda, it goes especially well with Ayurvedic medicines.

Even after reading this account of the advantages of Mudra Therapy, there are people who will remain sceptical. They will say, *"All this sounds too good to be true. Does Mudra Therapy really help ? Or is it all in the mind ? Perhaps mudras help because the performer strongly believes that they will. Without the performer's faith, mudras would fall flat on their faces."* Most people entertaining such doubts are scientists, especially doctors, who are self-appointed guardians of medical therapies and who have voluntarily taken upon themselves the responsibility of accusing anything that is unconventional. They fail to realize that a doctor should owe his responsibility to the patient alone and not to any system. We will say that :

(a) Mudras help people who are entirely new to, or unaware of, Mudra Therapy and have never witnessed its efficacy to become 'believers',

(b) Mudras help young children and even insane people, where the question of belief does not arise and

(c) Mudras even help semi-conscious or unconscious people (on whom Mudra Therapy is carried out passively by using rubber bands to maintain thumbs and fingers in specific positions).

And even if mudras were a placebo (a medicine/ therapy that works only because the patient believes in it), would it not be better and safer to regain health through belief rather than by resorting to medicines?

It is the clinical experience of numerous doctors and researchers that mudras are truely effective. They vouch for their usefulness. However, the reader should understand that Mudra Therapy is not a panacea or a 'cure-all'. Among all therapeutic sciences, there is not one form of treatment which does not have its limitations. And Mudra Therapy is no exception. All forms of treatment, medical or non-medical, are the brain-children of man. Man himself is imperfect. Therefore, any therapeutic system invented by man should, necessarily, be imperfect.

Mudra Therapy has no role to play in the treatment of the following disorders :

(1) Purely mechanical disorders like mature cataract, a big hole in the ear-drum, deviated nasal septum, cleft palate, hare lip, heart-valvular defects, varicose veins, hernias, big stones in the gall bladder/ urinary tract, prolapsed uterus / rectum / intervertebral disc, fracture, etc. These disorders will, obviously, need surgical intervention.

(2) Ailments caused by deficiences of nutrients, vitamins, minerals, etc.

(3) Disorders that are a part and parcel of old age (senile degeneration).

(4) Life-threatening ailments like cancer, AIDS, encephalitis, diptheria, heart failure, kidney failure, cirrhosis of the liver, septicaemia, gangrene, etc. These ailments call for strong, extreme measures rather than gentle mudras.

In conclusion, we will say that Mudra Therapy is an excellent key to try in the lock of disease. More often than not, it succeeds in opening up the lock. This key should, certainly, be tried when other keys (e.g., modern medicines) have either failed or are undesirable/ unapplicable. You may say that Mudra Therapy seems too simple to be really effective. We will say that in life, most important truths are, indeed, quite simple !

2. HOW DO MUDRAS HELP ?

The universe is composed of five basic elements : **space (or ether), air, fire, water and earth.** In Ayurvedic terminology, these are called **aakaash, vaayu, agni, jal and prithvi,** respectively. Being a miniature universe, the human body, too, is composed of the same five elements.

Each of these five elements serves a specific and important function within the body :

(1) **Aakaash (space)** is an inactive element that manifests itself in the bodily cavities like the cranial cavity, the paranasal sinuses, the ear cavity, the buccal cavity (mouth), the thoracic cavity, the abdomeno-pelvic cavity and the spaces within tubular/bag-like organs. Aakaash creates room within the body so that the rest of the elements can act. Aakaash is also associated with sound and, therefore, hearing. Ear ailments (e.g., acute pain) are relieved by the manipulation of Aakaash element.

(2) **Vaayu (air)** is the element of movement. All movements : of the body and within the body, voluntary as well as involuntary, are effected by air. Air is also responsible for our thoughts and emotions and for the movement of electrical impulses along sensory and motor nerves. Air is related to the sense of touch and, therefore, to the skin. Disorders of movements (lacking as in paralysis or excessive as in Parkinson's disease) can be helped by the manipulation of air element.

(3) **Agni (fire)** element is responsible for the body-temperature and metabolism. Fire works on the alimentary system, causing thirst, hunger, digestion of food and assimilation of digested food. Fire is also associated with vision and, therefore, eyes. Disorders like loss of appetite, indigestion and fatness can be helped by the manipulation (reinforcement) of the fire element.

(4) **Jal (water)** element is the constituent of protoplasm (the jelly-like substance present within cells), blood, tears, saliva, digestive juices, sweat, urine, semen, cerebro-spinal fluid (CSF) and fat. Water is also related to taste and, therefore, the tongue. Without water, the tongue cannot recognise various tastes. Disorders of water-metabolism within the body (e.g., dehydration or water-retention) can be helped by manipulating the water element.

(5) **Prithvi (earth)** element is the constituent of skin, hair, nails, bones, cartilage, muscles, etc. It is responsible for the body-mass. An excess of earth element causes obesity (overweight) whereas a deficiency causes emaciation (weight-loss). Earth is also associated with smell and, therefore, the nose. Disorders like leanness, prostration, debility, low immunity, etc., can be helped by the manipulation (reinforcement) of the earth element.

Good health is the natural consequence of a balanced and controlled functioning of each of these five elements. An excess or a deficiency of any one or more of these elements undermines health and causes disease.

Moreover, the five basic elements mentioned above, manifest in the human body as three basic principles or humors : **Vaata, Pitta and Kapha** as described in Ayurveda, the ancient Indian science of life, health and medicine.

Air and **space** elements, together, create the **Vaata humor**,

Fire and **Water** elements, together, create the **Pitta humor** whereas

Earth and **water** elements, together, create the **Kapha humor**.

Each of these three humors, Vaata, Pitta and Kapha exhibits certain properties (attributes) and performs vital functions in the body as described below :

Attributes of the three humors

Vaata	Pitta	Kapha
Light	Light	Heavy
Subtle	Subtle	Slimy, sticky
Mobile	Mobile	Static, slow
Cold	Hot	Cold
Dry	Moist, oily	Moist, oily
Rough	Sharp	Smooth

Functions of the three humors

Vaata	Pitta	Kapha
Movement	Body-heat	Stability
Breathing	Temperature	Energy
Natural urges	Digestion	Lubrication
Transformation of tissues	Perception	Unctuousness
Motor functions	Understanding	Forgiveness
Sensory functions	Hunger	Greed
Ungroundedness	Thirst	Attachment
Secretions	Intelligence	Accumulation
Excretions	Anger	Holding
Fear	Hatred	Possessiveness
Emptiness	Jealousy	
Anxiety		

A balance between these three humors is vital for good health; imbalance of any one or more results in disease. In present times, a perfect balance of these three humors is seldom seen. Due to hereditary factors, generally one humor dominates the other two right from birth, giving the person a **prakruti** or a **constitution.** For example, a person who has an excess of vaata humor in his body is said to be possessing a **Vaata-constitution** or suffering from **Vaata-dosha** (dosha = fault or imbalance). Similarly, people having an excess of Pitta humor or Kapha humor in their bodies are said to be possessing **pitta constitution** or **kapha constitution**, respectively. Such 'dosha' develops specific traits and susceptibilities in the owner, rendering him prone to certain diseases.

It may also happen that two (or sometimes all three) humors are deranged (i.e., in excess). Such people are said to be having mix constitutions. General features of each of these three basic constitutions have been elaborated below.

Vaata constitution

People of vaata constitution are, in general, physically underdeveloped. Their chests are flat and their veins, muscle-fibres and tendons are visible. The complexion is brown, the skin is cold, rough, dry and cracked. There usually are a few moles present, which tend to be dark.

Vaata people generally are either too tall or too short, with thin frames which reveal prominent joints and bone-ends because of poor muscle development. The hair is curly and scanty, the eyelashes are thin and the eyes lustreless. The eyes may be sunken, small, dry, active and the conjunctiva is dry and muddy. The nails are rough and brittle. The shape of the nose is bent and turned up.

Physiologically, the appetite and digestion are variable. Vaata people crave sweet, sour and salty tastes and like hot drinks. The production of urine is scanty and the stools are dry, hard and small in quantity. They have a tendency to perspire less than other constitutional types. Their sleep may be disturbed and they will sleep less than the other types. Their hands and feet are often cold.

These people are creative, active, alert and restless. They talk fast and walk fast but they are easily fatigued.

Psychologically, they are characterized by short memory but quick mental understanding. They will understand something immediately, but will soon forget it. They have little will-power, tend toward mental instability and possess little tolerance, confidence or boldness. Their reasoning power is weak and these people are nervous, fearful and afflicted by much anxiety.

Each constitutional type also exhibits certain patterns in interactions with the external environment. Vaata people tend to earn money quickly and also to spend it quickly. Thus, they tend to remain poor.

People having a Vaata constitution are prone to diseases listed under Vaayu-shaamak, Vaata-naashak and Apaan-vaayu mudras

Pitta constitution

These people are of medium height, are slender and their body-frame may be delicate. Their chests are not as flat as those of vaata people and they show a medium prominence of veins and muscle tendons. They have many moles or freckles which are bluish or brownish-red. The bones are not as prominent as in the vaata individual. Muscle development is moderate.

The pitta complexion may be coppery, yellowish, reddish or fair. The skin is soft, warm and less wrinkled than vaata skin. The hair is thin, silky, red or brownish and there is a tendency toward premature graying/loss of hair. The eyes may be gray, green or copper-brown and sharp; the eyeballs are of medium prominence. The conjuctiva is moist and copper-colored. The nails are soft. The shape of the nose is sharp and the tip tends to be reddish.

Physiologically, these people have a strong metabolism, good digestion and therefore, strong appetites. The person of pitta constitution usually takes large quantities of food and liquid. Pitta types have a natural craving for sweet, bitter and astringent tastes and enjoy cold drinks. Their sleep is of medium duration but uninterrupted. They produce a large volume of urine and the stools are yellowish, liquid, soft and plentiful. There is a tendency toward excessive perspiring. The body-temperature may run slightly high and hands and feet tend to be warm. Pitta people do not tolerate sunlight, heat or hard work.

Psychologically, pitta people have a good power of comprehension; they are very intelligent and sharp and tend to be good orators. They have emotional tendencies toward hate, anger and jealousy.

They are ambitious people who generally like to be leaders. Pitta people appreciate material prosperity and they tend to be moderately well-off financially. They enjoy exhibiting their wealth and luxurious possessions.

People having a pitta constitution are prone to diseases listed under the Prithvi-vardhak, Pitta-shaamak and Shankh mudras.

Kapha constitution

People of kapha constitution have well-developed bodies. There is, however, a strong tendency for these individuals to carry excess weight. Their chests are expanded and broad. The veins and tendons of kapha people are not obvious because of their thick skin and their muscle development is good. The bones are not prominent.

Their complexion is fair and bright. The skin is soft, lustrous and oily; it is also cold and pale. The hair is thick, dark, soft and wavy. The eyes are dense and black or blue; the white of the eye is generally very white, large and attractive. The conjuctiva does not tend to redness.

Physiologically, kapha people have regular appetites, the digestion functions relatively slowly and there is less intake of food. They tend to move slowly. They crave pungent, bitter and astringent foods. Stools are soft and may be pale in colour; evacuation is slow. Their perspiration is moderate. Sleep is sound and prolonged. There is a strong vital capacity evidenced by good stamina, and kapha people are generally healthy, happy and peaceful.

Psychologically, they tend to be tolerant, calm, forgiving and loving; however, they also exhibit traits of greed, attachment, envy and possessiveness. Their comprehension is slow but definite; once they understand something, that knowledge is retained.

Kapha people tend to be wealthy. They earn money and are good at holding on to it.

People having a kapha constitution are prone to develop diseases listed under the Prithvi-shaamak, Kapha-shaamak and Linga mudras.

The general features of the three individual constitutions have been described above. However, it is often seen that people have mix (compound) constitutions, e.g.,

(1) Vaata + Pitta constitution, where both V and P are in excess,

(2) Vaata + Kapha constitution, where both V and K are in excess,

(3) Pitta + Kapha constitution, where both P and K are in excess and

(4) Vaata + Pitta + Kapha constitution, where all the three humors are at fault (hence called Tridosha).

To be able to derive the fullest advantage of this book, we advise you, dear reader, to correctly judge your own individual constitution with the help of the table given in the following pages. Without this understanding, you will not be able to select the correct mudra(s) for overcoming your present illnesses or preventing the future ones.

In the table, 24 features of each humor are described. At the left of each feature is provided a box □. You should write within each box the letter V (for Vaata) or P (for Pitta) or K (for Kapha), whichever seems appropriate for you. If you cannot decide on a particular feature, write V (because Vaata people are naturally indecisive !). After finishing the test, count how many V's, P's and K's you have got. This will give you your constitution. Please also refer to the note given at the end of the table.

Features	Vaata	Pitta	Kapha
□ Mind, Nature	Great initiative; Fast speed of work; however, cannot sustain efforts	Moderate initiative;	Lacks enthusiasm; slow speed of work; however, can work tirelessly
	Timid, fearful, indecisive, impatient (restless), moody, unreliable	Irritable, angry, proud, quarrelsome, jealous	Calm, patient, reliable
	Very few friends	Few friends	Many friends

☐ Memory	Poor	Moderate	Excellent
☐ Reaction to temperature / weather	Ailments worse in autumn. Intolerance of wind and cold climate. Liking for sunshine, warmth.	Ailments worse in summer. Intolerance of heat. Liking for cool weather.	Ailments worse in spring and monsoon. Intolerance of dampness and humidity. Liking for warmth.
☐ Sensitivity	Intolerance of pain, noise	Intolerance of stress, noise	Intolerance of fast-life
☐ Stamina / Endurance	Low	Medium	Excellent
☐ Body-frame	Lean, short or tall, light-weight. Weight hard to gain, easy to lose	Moderately built yet delicate. Weight stable	Broad, heavy, fleshy Weight easy to gain, hard to lose.
☐ Head-size	Small	Medium	Large
☐ Face	Small forehead Thin eyebrows. Big, restless, muddy eyes Thin, unequal lips.	Medium forehead Medium eyebrows. Yellow, piercing eyes that turn red from anger, sunshine or alcohol; Lips red	Broad forehead Thick bushy eyebrows Big, white, lusterous eyes; Lips thick and moist
☐ Speech and voice	Voice feeble, hoarse; speech unsteady, faltering, stammering	Voice clear; speech sharp, cutting	Voice sweet, soft, loud and clear
☐ Gait (walk)	Quick, irregular noisy	Stable	Slow
☐ Movements	short and fast; tremors, shivering	sharp and precise	slow and steady
☐ Hunger	Irregular, frequent, excessive	strong; cannot undertake a fast	Less, but can eat a lot; can also undertake a fast

☐ Liking for	Hot foods and drinks	sweets; cold foods and drinks	Hot, spicy, bitter foods; dry foods
☐ Digestion	unreliable	strong and fast; burning in digestive tract	strong and slow
☐ Stools	Irregular evacuation; constipation, flatulence (gas)	Multiple, yellow, loose, bulky; sometimes bloody	Regular evacuation. Stools well formed; occasionally mucous–laden
☐ Thirst	Capricious, less	Excessive; desires cold water	Normal
☐ Urine	Scanty, difficult	yellow, red, hot burning	Pale, profuse, milky
☐ Sweat	Little, if at all	Profuse, foul-smelling	Little
☐ Sleep	Light, interrupted with eyes half open; Grinds teeth in sleep	Moderate	Long and sound
☐ Dreams	Trees, mountains, running, jumping, flying	sun, fire, lightning, violence	water, lakes, birds
☐ Menses	Irregular, scanty, painful; blood dark	Excessive, painful; blood bright red	Moderate with heaviness in abdomen; blood pale
☐ Skin	Cold, dry, cracked; Nails brittle; complexion dark	Hot, yellow or red (rashes), mature	Cold, delicate; there may be itching without rashes.
☐ Hair	Dry, rough, curly	Soft, sparce, balding; premature greying	Long, dense, oily
☐ Joints	Loose, creaking; Prominent, projecting bones	Moderately strong, hot, reddish	Firm, stable, covered by flesh

Note :

If you have many more V's than P's or K's, you have a Vaata constitution.

If you have many more P's than V's or K's, you have a Pitta constitution.

If you have many more K's than V's or P's, you have a Kapha constitution.

If you have more and (almost) equal V's and P's, you have a Vaata + Pitta constitution.

If you have more and (almost) equal V's and K's, you have a Vaata + Kapha constitution.

If you have more and (almost) equal P's and K's, you have a Pitta + Kapha constitution.

If you have more or less equal V's, P's and K's you have Tridosha (Tri = three, dosha = faults).

The question posed in the title of this chapter, **'How do mudras help ?'** still remains unanswered. We will reply by saying that when correctly chosen and diligently practised, **mudras restore a state of balance to the five elements and pacify the aggravated humor/s**. Thereby, a true well-being is regained.

There are a number of methods of balancing the elements and/or humor/s. These include bringing about changes in life-style and/or diet, taking Ayurvedic medicines or practising mudras. Among these methods, Mudra Therapy is most simple, quite easy and costs nothing.

The five fingers of each hand represent the five elements.

Fire resides in the **thumb,**

Air resides in the **index finger,**

Space resides in the **middle finger,**

Earth resides in the **ring finger** and

Water resides in the **little finger.**

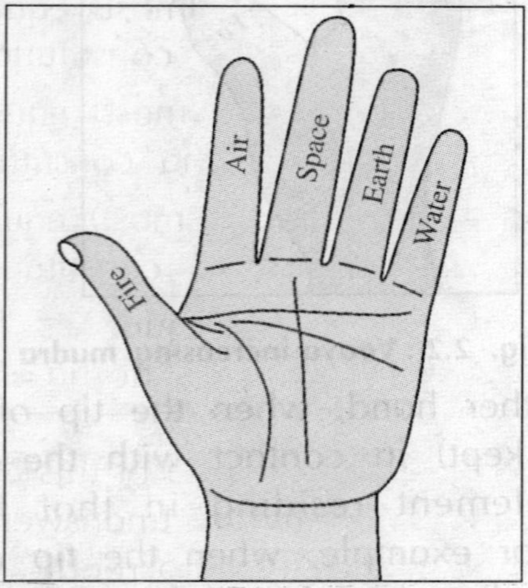

Fig. 2.1

The thumb is the most important among the five digits of a hand, controlling the rest of the four fingers. Similarly, fire is the most important among the five elements, being able to control the remaining four.

According to principles of Mudra Therapy and the clinical experiences of innumerable Ayurvedic physicians, when the tip of a finger is brought (and kept) in contact with the tip of the thumb, the element residing in that finger starts increasing. For example, when the tip of the index finger is brought (and kept) in contact with the thumb-tip (forming the Gyaan-mudra), the element Vaayu (air) starts increasing (see figure 2.2).

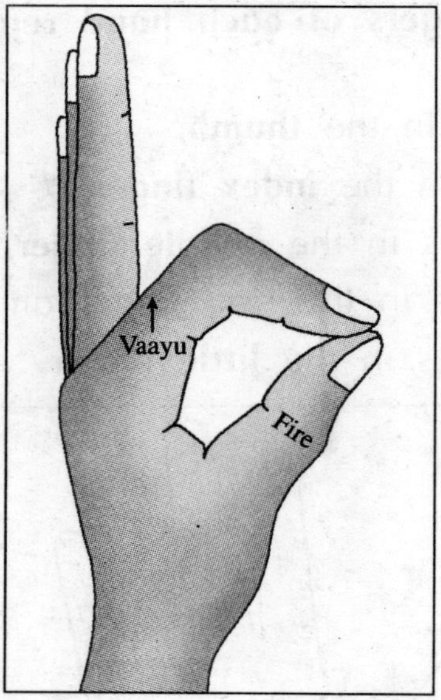

Fig. 2.2 : Vaayu-increasing mudra

On the other hand, when the tip of a finger is brought (and kept) in contact with the base of the thumb, the element residing in that finger starts diminishing. For example, when the tip of the index finger is touched to the base of the thumb (to form the Vaayu mudra), the element Vaayu (air) starts decreasing (see figure 2.3).

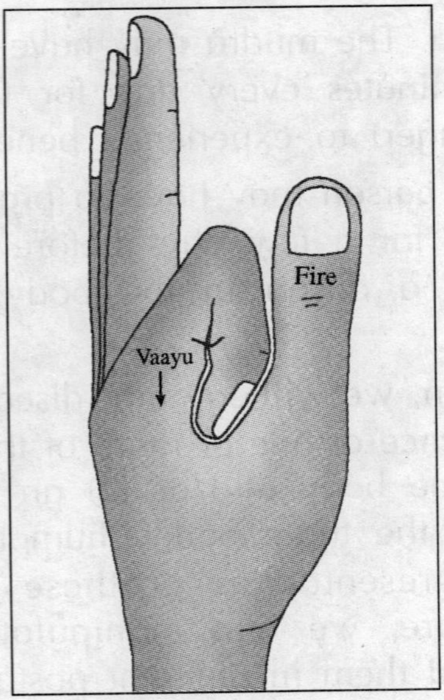

Fig. 2.3 : Vaayu-decreasing mudra

Note : Since the elements fire and earth have qualities opposed to each other, when the tip of the ring finger is touched to the thumb-tip, the element earth residing in the ring finger increases at the cost of the element fire residing in the thumb; however, when the tip of the ring finger is touched to the base of the thumb, the element earth decreases but the element fire increases.

This change (i.e., increase or decrease) in the level of an element, sometimes begins almost immediately; at other times it may take 45 minutes or longer. For example, acute ear-pain resulting from an increase of element space in the body (ear) can be relieved within minutes of performing Aakaash-shaamak (Shunya) mudra; similarly, acute chest-pain due to heart disease can be quickly helped by performing Apaan-vaayu mudra. However, other (especially chronic) diseases may not, necessarily, be immediately helped on performing a suitable mudra. The mudra may have to be practised for about 45 minutes every day for fifteen days (or occasionally longer) to experience benefits.

Similarly, a person may have to practise a suitable mudra regularly for a few days before an aggravated humor (causing a dosha in the body) starts getting pacified.

In conclusion, we will say that diseases are caused by (1) an imbalance of one or more of the five elements that constitute the body and/or (2) an aggravation of one or more of the three bodily humors. Fingers and thumbs are representatives of these elements and humors. Therefore, we can manipulate fingers and thumbs (i.e., hold them in different postures or mudras) to rebalance and regulate the elements and humors and, thereby, restore health.

3. GENERAL GUIDELINES FOR MUDRA THERAPY

(1) Touching a finger-tip to the thumb-tip increases the element residing in that finger whereas touching a finger-tip to the thumb-base reduces the element residing in that finger.

(2) When performing a mudra, a light contact between the thumb and the finger/s is sufficient; firm pressure is not really required.

(3) When performing a mudra, the position of other fingers (which are not participating in that mudra) is immaterial. They can be held (effortlessly) straight or allowed to bend as per the practitioner's desire or convenience. Both the figures shown below constitute the same mudra : Vaayu-vardhak or Gyaan mudra.

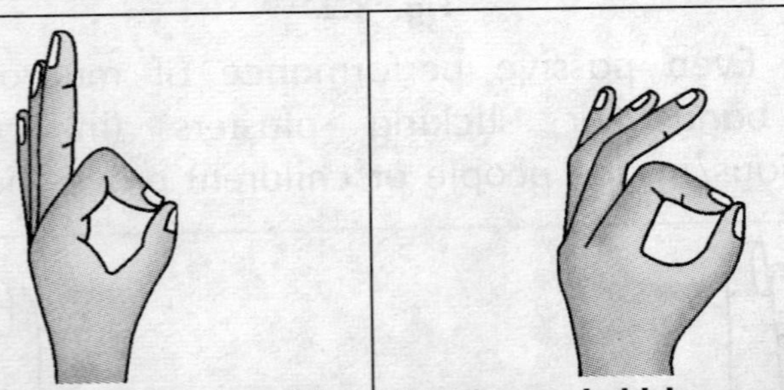

(a) Fingers held stiff and straight | **(b) Fingers held loose and bent**

Fig. 3.1

(4) Whenever possible, perform mudras with both the hands.

(5) Mudras can be practised anytime, anywhere e.g., while reading a newspaper in the morning, while travelling to the office or back home, while watching T.V. or listening to music, etc. However, simultaneous meditation can, perhaps yield greater benefits.

(6) Mudras can be performed in any body-position i.e., lying, sitting, standing, walking, etc. However, simultaneous meditational asanas like Padmasana or Vajrasana are recommended.

Fig. 3.2

(7) Even passive performance of mudras, using rubber bands or sticking plasters (in cases of unconscious/insane people or children) proves beneficial.

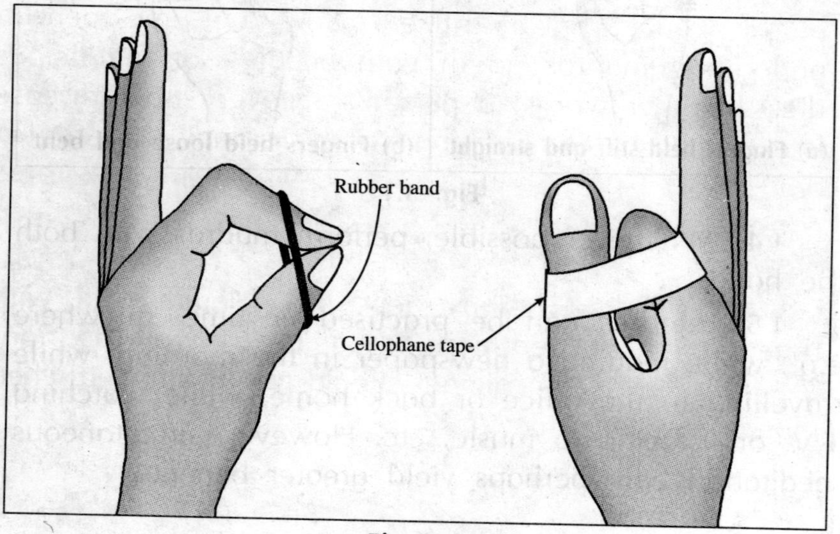

Fig. 3.3

(8) Only a few mudras (e.g., Aakaash-shaamak and Apaan-vaayu mudras) help within a few minutes of beginning to perform them. Rest of the mudras have to be practised for about 45 minutes every day (either at one stretch or in three parts, each of 15 minutes), for at least 15 days to experience benefits. In fact they should be practised till the disease is eradicated, however long it takes.

(9) *'Should a person undergoing Mudra Therapy bring about changes in diet?'*, is a question that is frequently asked. We will say that though not indispensable, suitable dietary changes can reinforce the benefits of mudras whereas unsuitable diet can, at least partially, offset the good effects of mudras. If a person having an excess of element Vaayu (air) or humor Vaata in his body liberally consumes foods that can increase Vaayu or Vaata, he may not benefit (or may benefit only partially and slowly) even by a most religious and regular practice of suitable (i.e., Vaayu-decreasing or Vaata-decreasing) mudra/s. Quite obviously, no sane person would want his sincere efforts and time spent in performing mudras go in vain because of injudicious diet. In other words, a person's recovery from disease is expedited by combinining Mudra Therapy with correct diet. Suggestions about appropriate diet for the three constitutional types, Vaata, Pitta and Kapha, have been presented in Appendix 1, at the end of this book.

(10) Mudra Therapy goes along quite well with other forms of treatment, medical as well as non-medical. Previous medicines should not be stopped when beginning Mudra Therapy.

SECTION II

4. THERAPEUTIC MUDRAS

(1) Vaayu-vardhak (वायु-वर्धक) or Gyan mudra

Popularly known as **Gyaan (Gnaan/Dnyaan) mudra,** this mudra increases the vaayu (**air**) element within the body.

Method : This mudra is formed by joining together, the tip of the index finger with the tip of the thumb.

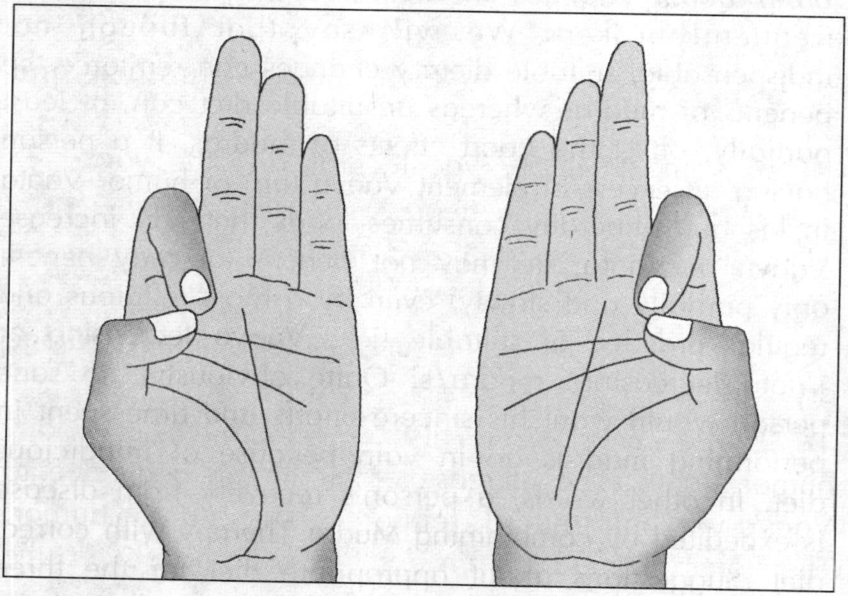

Fig. 4.1

Effects : Vaayu-vardhak mudra increases the vaayu (air) element within the body. Thus reinforced, the air –

(1) empowers the mind, causing a positive effect on emotions and leading to enlightenment,

(2) empowers the nervous system (including the brain),

(3) facilitates movements of electrical impulses along nerves,

(4) empowers the pituitary gland and, thereby, the entire system of endocrine glands,

(5) empowers muscles, both voluntary and involuntary,

(6) empowers the vocal cords and the voice,

(7) empowers the heart, increasing its efficiency,

(8) renders the skin and the mucous membranes dry,

(9) renders the joints and the articular cartilage dry.

The element Air is also a component of bodily humor Vaata. The increase of air in the body due to Vaayu-vardhak mudra reinforces the Vaata humor. Therefore, this mudra is an excellent mudra to overcome Vaata-deficiency. However, it should be practised in moderation by people who already have a Vaata constitution (i.e., an excess of Vaata in their bodies).

Benefits : Vaayu-vardhak mudra can be used to treat the following disorders :

(1) Dullness of mind, lack of enthusiasm-initiative-creativity, recklessness, loss of memory,

(2) Drowsiness, lethargy, mental retardation,

(3) Disorders of the nervous system like cerebral palsy, neuritis, neuropathies, Alzheimer's disease, Tabes dorsalis, multiple sclerosis, motor neurone disease, Ataxias, Dementias, Syringomyelia, etc.,

(4) Degeneration of the retina, optic atrophy,

(5) Endocrine (hormonal) disorders like hypopituitarism (causing dwarfism, Simmond's disease, Frohlick's syndrome), hypothyroidism (causing cretinism, myxoedema), hypoparathyroidism, hypoadrenalism (causing Addison's disease), diabetes, hypogonadism, etc.,

(6) Muscular disorders like myopathies, myesthenia gravis, paresis, paralysis (viz paralytic squint, ptosis, facial palsy, vocal paralysis, respiratory paralysis, monoplegia, paraplegia, hemiplegia, quadriplegia, etc.),

(7) Lost or feeble voice,

(8) Bradycardia (slow heart beats), weakness or gradual failure of the heart,

(9) Formation of excessive mucous in respiratory and/or digestive tracts,

(10) Effusion in joints.

Duration : 45 minutes every day, either at one stretch or in three parts (i.e., for 15 minutes, thrice a day).

Ideal time : Though Vaayu-vardhak mudra can be performed at any time of the day, practising it at anytime between 2.00 to 6.00 am/pm gives better results.

Precaution : People with a pronounced Vaata prakruti (constitution) should perform this mudra in moderation, if at all.

Some variations of Vaayu-vardhak or Gyaan mudra

Given below are some variations of Gyaan mudra, which, apart from yielding the benefits of Gyaan mudra, bestow some additional gains.

(a) Vairaagya (वैराग्य) mudra

This mudra enables the practitioner to gradually develop (1) a sense of detachment from worldly matters and (2) a realization about the futility of material gains.

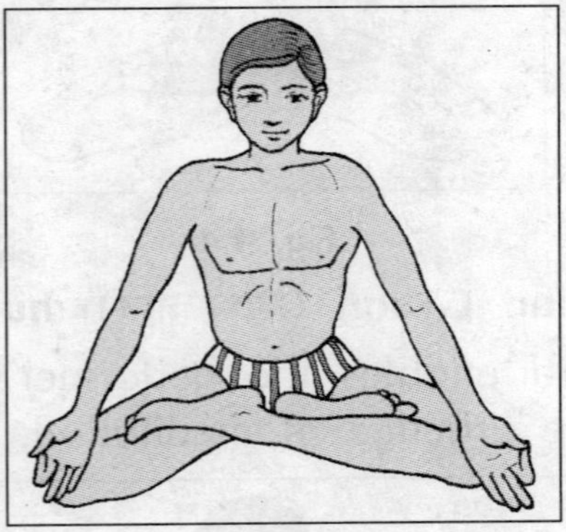

Fig. 4.2

(b) Purna Gyaan (पूर्ण ज्ञान) mudra

This mudra enables the practitioner to obtain complete knowledge or absolute truth about all matters.

Fig. 4.3

(c) Abhay Gyaan (अभय ज्ञान) mudra

This mudra enables the practitioner to develop the virtue of fearlessness.

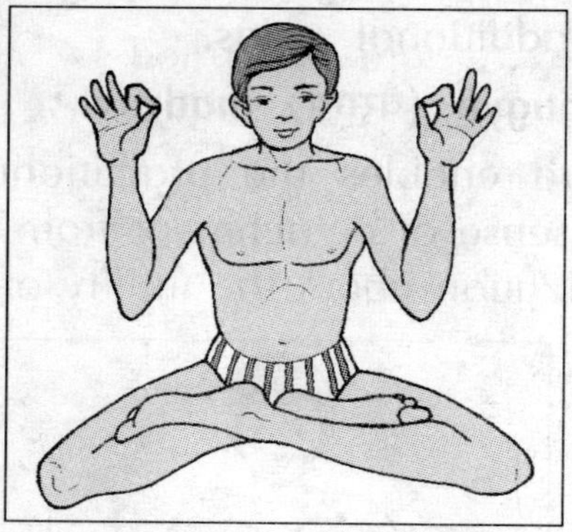

Fig. 4.4

(d) Dhyaan Gyaan (ध्यान ज्ञान) mudra

This mudra enables the performer to make rapid progress in the practice of meditation.

Fig. 4.5

(2) Vaayu-shaamak (वायु-शामक) or Vaayu mudra

Popularly known as **Vaayu mudra**, this mudra decreases the vaayu **(air)** element within the body.

Method : This mudra is formed by first placing the tip of the index finger on the base of the thumb and then bringing gentle pressure of the thumb upon this finger. This amounts to suppression of element air (residing in the first finger) by element fire (residing in the thumb).

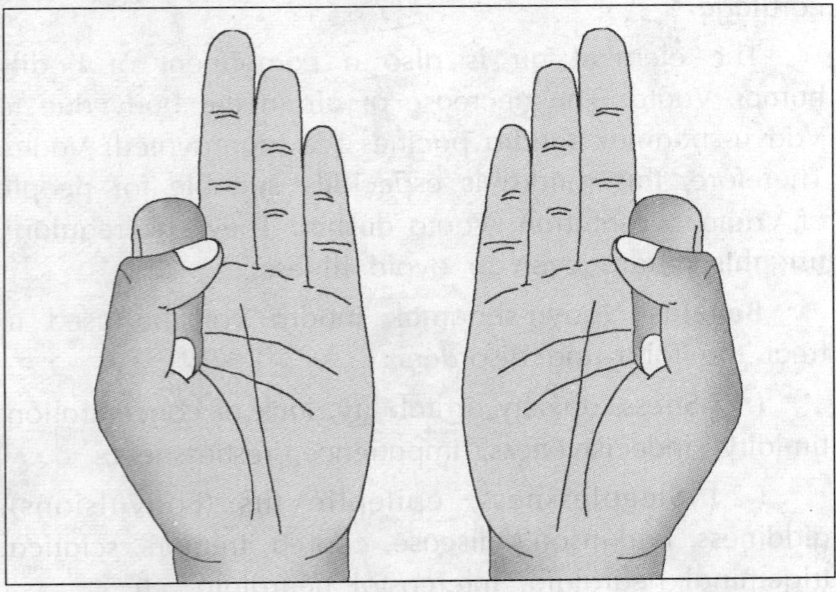

Fig. 4.6

Effects : Vaayu-shaamak mudra decreases the air element within the body. This reduction of air –

(1) sedates restless and anxious mind,

(2) calms overcharged nervous system,

(3) pacifies overactive endocrine glands,

(4) relaxes tense or spastic muscles,

(5) soothes strained voice,

(6) allows rehydration of skin and articular cartilage.

The element air is also a component of bodily humor Vaata. The decrease of air in the body due to Vaayu-shaamak mudra pacifies the (aggravated) Vaata. Therefore, this mudra is especially suitable for people of Vaata constitution (Vaata dosha). They can regularly use this mudra even to avoid illness.

Benefits : Vaayu-shaamak mudra can be used to treat the following disorders :

(1) Stress, anxiety, irritability, lack of concentration, timidity, indecisiveness, impatience, restlessness,

(2) Sleeplessness, epileptic fits (convulsions), giddiness, Parkinson's disease, chorea, tremors, sciatica, trigeminal neuralgia, intercostal neuralgia, etc.,

(3) Hormonal imbalances caused by overactivity of endocrine glands,

(4) Twitching of eye-lids, nystagmus (constant involuntary eye-movements),

(5) Tinnitus (noises in the ear/s), vertigo, dizziness,

(6) Breathlessness, tachycardia (fast heart beats), palpitations,

(7) Hiccups,

(8) Muscle-spasm, muscle-cramps, muscular rigidity,

(9) Crackling joints (Osteo-Arthritis), gout,

(10) Dry, rough skin/hair, brittle nails,

(11) Constipation, flatulence (gas formation).

Duration : 45 minutes every day either at one stretch or in 3 parts (i.e., for 15 minutes, thrice a day).

Ideal time : Though Vaayu-shaamak mudra can be done at any time of the day, practising it anytime other than 2.00 to 6.00 am/pm gives better results.

Precaution : Many experienced doctors say that the practice of this mudra should be discontinued as soon as the disease has been overcome.

(3) Aakaash-vardhak (आकाश-वर्धक) or Aakash mudra

Popularly known as **Aakaash mudra**, this mudra increases the (inactive) **Aakaash** (**ether** or **space**) element within the body.

Method : This mudra is formed by joining together the tips of the thumb and the middle finger.

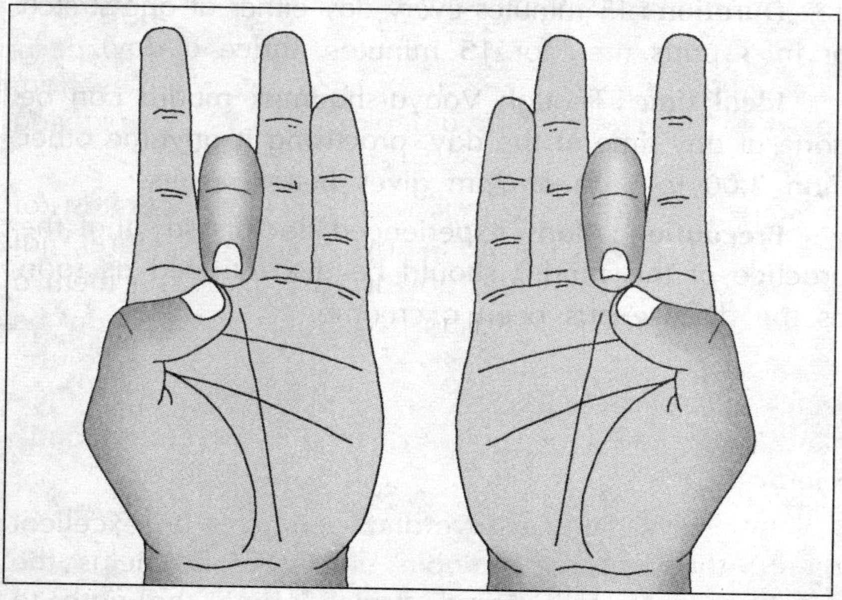

Fig. 4.7

Effects : Aakaash-vardhak mudra increases the aakaash (space) element within the body. Since the space within the body is a part of the outer space (aakaash or cosmos), practice of this mudra enables the individual (aatmaa) to reunite with the collective consciousness (Paramaatmaa or God). Negative emotions like fear, anger, sorrow, etc., are replaced by positive emotions and thoughts.

The above-mentioned increase in internal space is effected by the elimination of metabolic wastes from the body. Thus Aakaash-vardhak mudra is a detoxifying mudra.

The increased internal space enables the rest of the four bodily elements : vaayu (air), agni (fire), jal (water) and prithvi (earth) to increase, affording them a room to act. Thus, Aakaash-vardhak mudra can be beneficially combined with mudras that increase the other four elements (i.e., Vaayu-vardhak mudra, Prithvi-vardhak mudra, Agni-vardhak mudra and Jal-vardhak mudra).

In general, Aakaash-vardhak mudra is an excellent mudra that stimulates noble thoughts and helps the practitioner to take rapid strides along the path to moksha (salvation). It also helps a person who wishes to scale great heights in the art of meditation.

The element Aakaash is also a component of bodily humor Vaata. Therefore, Aakaash-vardhak mudra reinforces the Vaata humor of the body. It should be done in moderation by people of Vaata constitution.

Benefits : Practice of Aakaash-vardhak mudra helps –

(1) to develop noble, elevated thoughts,

(2) to develop intuition and extra sensory powers (ESP),

(3) to detoxify the body by the elimination of metabolic wastes (through exhaled air, sweat, urine and stools),

(4) to overcome a feeling of fullness / heaviness in the body or body-parts,

(5) to overcome discomfort caused by over-eating,

(6) to relieve congestion (and pain) in the head (due to migraine or sinusitis), ear / s (due to infection), chest (due to infection / asthma), etc.,

(7) High blood pressure, irregular heart-beats, angina pectoris, etc.

Duration : 45 minutes every day, either at one stretch or in three parts (i.e., for 15 minutes, thrice a day).

Ideal time : Though Aakaash vardhak mudra can be performed any time of the day, practising it at any-time between 2.00 to 6.00 am / pm gives better results.

Precaution : People with a pronounced Vaata prakruti (constitution) should perform this mudra in moderation, if at all.

(4) Aakaash-shaamak (आकाश-शामक) or Shoonya mudra

Popularly known as **Shoonya mudra**, this mudra decreases the **Aakaash (space)** element within the body.

Method : This mudra is formed by first placing the tip of the middle finger on the base of the thumb and then bringing gentle pressure of the thumb upon this finger. This amounts to suppression of element space (residing in the middle finger) by element fire (residing in the thumb).

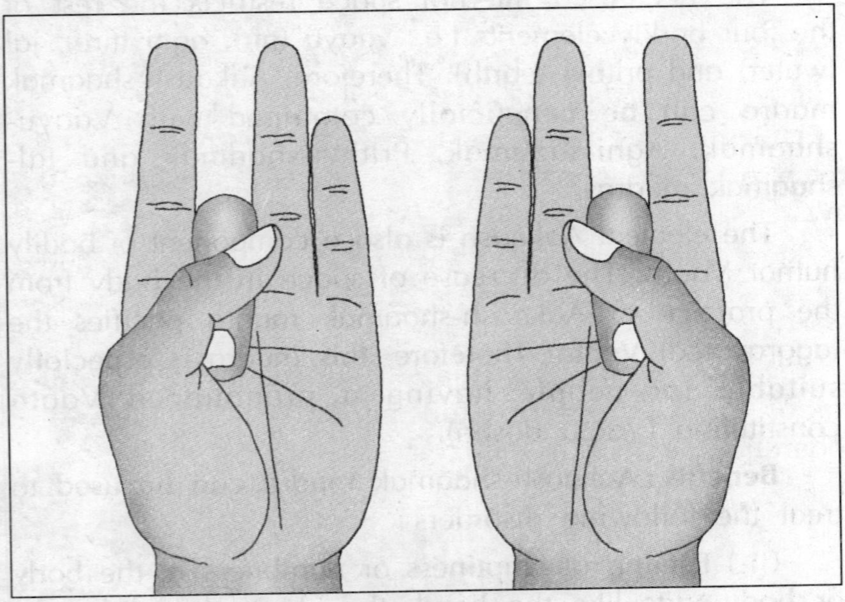

Fig. 4.8

Effects : Aakaash-shaamak mudra decreases the Aakaash (space) element within the body. It can, therefore, be used to treat disorders (enlisted below) caused by an abnormal increase of space within the body. The element space is associated with ears. Therefore, Aakaash-shaamak mudra helps certain ear disorders. In fact, it is an almost failproof remedy for ear-pain.

The decreased internal space restricts the rest of the four bodily elements i.e., vaayu (air), agni (fire), jal (water) and prithvi (earth). Therefore, Aakaash-shaamak mudra can be beneficially combined with Vaayu-shaamak, Agni-shaamak, Prithvi-shaamak and Jal-shaamak mudras.

The element Aakaash is also a component of bodily humor Vaata. The decrease of space in the body from the practice of Aakaash-shaamak mudra pacifies the (aggravated) Vaata. Therefore, this mudra is especially suitable for people having a pronounced Vaata constitution (Vaata dosha).

Benefits : Aakaash-shaamak mudra can be used to treat the following disorders :

(1) Feeling of emptiness or numbness in the body or body-parts like the head, the chest, the abdomen, etc.,

(2) Ear ailments like pain, tinnitus (noises), vertigo and acquired deafness.

Duration : In case of acute ear-pain, incapacitating vertigo or severe numbness, perform this mudra continuously till the disorder subsides. For chronic ear-ailments or numbness peform this mudra for 45 minutes either at one stretch or in 3 parts (i.e., for 15 minutes, thrice a day).

Ideal time : For chronic diseases, this mudra should, if possible, be performed at anytime other than 2.00 to 6.00 am / pm gives better results.

Precaution : Experienced doctors believe that the practice of this mudra should be discontinued as soon as the disease has been overcome.

(5) Prithvi-vardhak (पृथ्वी-वर्धक) or Prithvi mudra

Popularly known as **Prithvi mudra**, this mudra increases the **Prithvi (earth)** element within the body. At the same time, it decreases the **Agni (fire)** element. Therefore, it can also be called **Agni-shaamak mudra.**

Method : This mudra is formed by joining together the tips of the ring finger and the thumb.

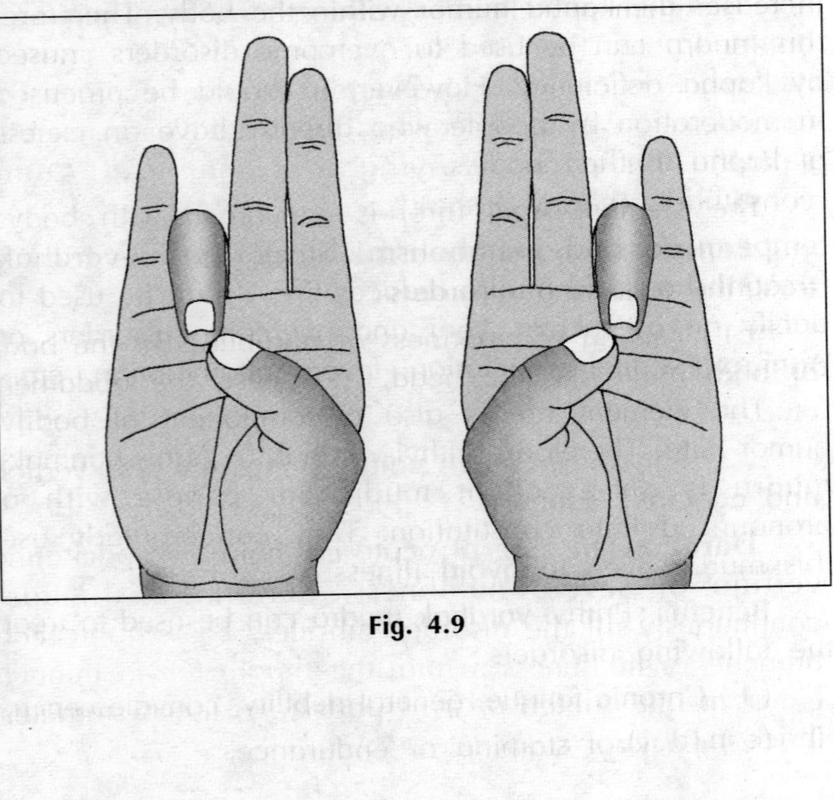

Fig. 4.9

Effects : Prithvi-vardhak mudra increases the Prithvi (earth) element within the body but decreases the Agni (fire) element within the body.

The element earth is a vital component of bodily tissues like bones, cartilage, skin, hair, nails, flesh, muscles, tendons, internal organs, etc. Practice of Prithvi-vardhak mudra builds and invigorates these tissues. In other words, this mudra increases vitality, strength and endurance.

The element earth is also associated with the nose (smell). Therefore, Prithvi-vardhak mudra can be used to overcome nasal disorders (e.g., loss of sense of smell).

The element earth is also a component of the bodily humor kapha. Practice of Prithvi-vardhak mudra increases the kapha humor within the body. Therefore, this mudra can be used to overcome disorders caused by kapha deficiency. However, it should be practised in moderation by people who already have an excess of kapha in their bodies.

The element Agni (fire) is concerned with body-temperature and metabolism. Since Prithvi-vardhak (= Agni-shaamak) mudra reduces fire, it can be used to pacify an overactive Agni and overcome disorders of Agni-excess like emaciation, fever, inflammation, etc.

The element fire is also a component of bodily humor Pitta. Therefore, Prithvi-vardhak (= Agni-shaamak) mudra is an excellent mudra for people with a pronounced Pitta constitution. They can regularly use this mudra even to avoid illness.

Benefits : Prithvi-vardhak mudra can be used to treat the following disorders :

(1) Chronic fatigue, general debility, convalescence,

(2) Lack of stamina or endurance,

(3) Inexplicable weight-loss, emaciation,

(4) Osteoporosis osteomalacia (diminished bone-density), rickets,

(5) Fracture (to expedite union),

(6) Degeneration of articular cartilage (Osteo-Arthritis),

(7) Weak, atrophied muscles, myopathies,

(8) Paresis, paralysis, poliomyelitis,

(9) Dry, cracked, burning, mature skin,

(10) Skin-rashes, urticaria,

(11) Brittle nails,

(12) Hair-loss, premature greying of hair,

(13) Burning in eyes, stomach (acidity), urine, anus, hands, feet, head,

(14) Aphthous ulcers in the mouth,

(15) Ulcers in the stomach, intestines,

(16) Inflammatory diseases (diseases whose names end with 'itis'),

(17) Jaundice,

(18) Fever,

(19) Hyperthyroidism.

Duration : 45 minutes every day, either at one stretch or in 3 parts (i.e., for 15 minutes, thrice a day). However, people with kapha deficiency can do it even for longer periods.

Ideal time : Though Prithvi-vardhak mudra can be performed at anytime of the day, practising it at anytime between 6.00 to 10.00 am / pm gives better results.

Precaution : People with a pronounced kapha constitution should perform this mudra in moderation, if at all.

(6) Prithvi-shaamak (पृथ्वी-शामक) or Surya mudra

Popularly known as **Surya mudra**, this mudra increases the **Agni (fire)** element within the body. It can, therefore, be called **Agni-vardhak mudra**, too. At the same time, this mudra decreases the **Prithvi (earth)** element within the body.

Method : This mudra is formed by first placing the tip of the ring finger on the base of the thumb and then bringing gentle pressure of the thumb upon this finger. This amounts to suppression of element earth (residing in the ring finger) by element fire (residing in the thumb). The earth element thus suppressed, fire is able to rage unopposed.

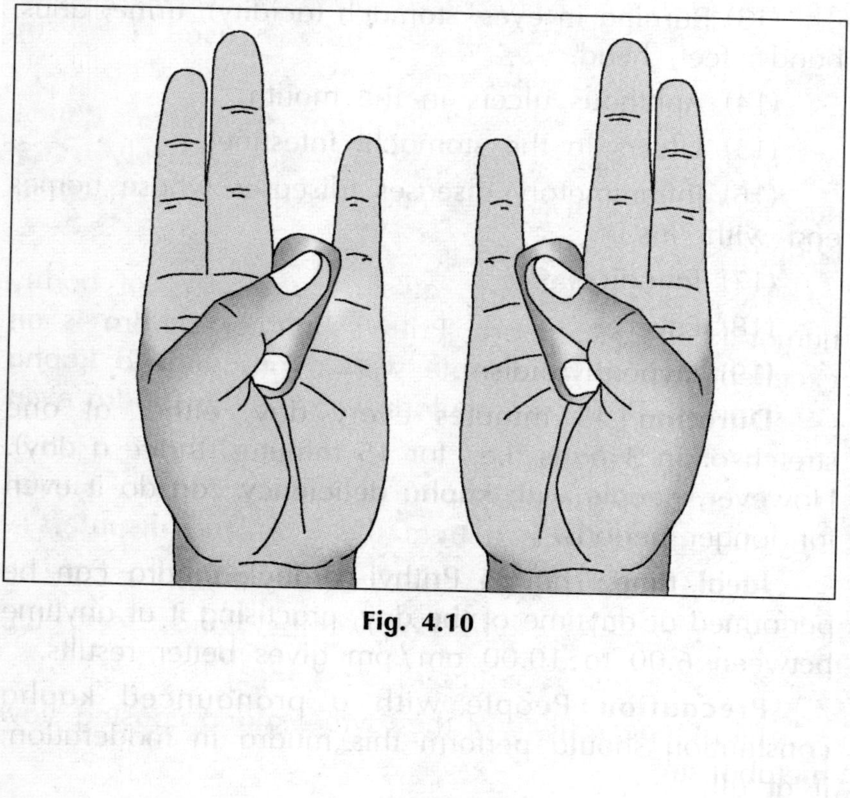

Fig. 4.10

Effects : Prithvi-shaamak or Agni-vardhak mudra increases the Agni (fire) element within the body but subdues the Prithvi (earth) element.

The element Agni (fire) is associated with body-temperature and metabolism. Practice of Prithvi-shaamak or Surya mudra helps to maintain the body-temperature and keeps the metabolism going.

The element Agni is also connected with vision. Hence, regular practice of Surya mudra helps to strengthen weak eyes and improve vision.

Agni is also a component of bodily humor Pitta. Practice of Prithvi-shaamak or Surya mudra increases the Pitta humor within the body. Therefore, this mudra can be used to overcome disorders caused by Pitta deficiency. However, it should be used only in moderation by people having an excess of Pitta.

Prithvi-shaamak mudra decreases the element Prithvi (earth) within the body. It is, therefore, excellent for people having an excess of element Prithvi in their bodies.

The element earth is also a component of bodily humor kapha. Therefore, Prithvi-shaamak mudra is an excellent mudra for people with a pronounced kapha constitution. They can regularly practise this mudra even to prevent illness.

Benefits : Prithvi-shaamak (Agni-vardhak; Surya) mudra can be used to treat the following disorders :

(1) Abnormally low body-temperature,

(2) Coldness of skin, body, limbs, hands, feet, etc.,

(3) Intolerance to cold, shivering,

(4) Underactivity of the thyroid gland causing slow metabolism,

(5) Obesity, progressive weight-gain,

(6) Loss of appetite, indigestion, constipation,

(7) Absence of sweating,

(8) Certain vision / eye problems, especially cataract.

Duration : 45 minutes every day either at one stretch or in 3 parts (i.e., for 15 minutes, thrice a day).

Ideal time : Though this mudra can be performed any time, practising it at anytime from 10 am to 2 pm or 10 pm to 2 am gives better results.

Precaution : Over-performance of this mudra may cause undue heating of the body.

(7) Jal-vardhak (जल-वर्धक) or Varun mudra

Popularly known as **Varun** mudra, this mudra increases the **Jal** (water) element within the body.

Method : This mudra is formed by joining together the tips of the thumb and the little finger.

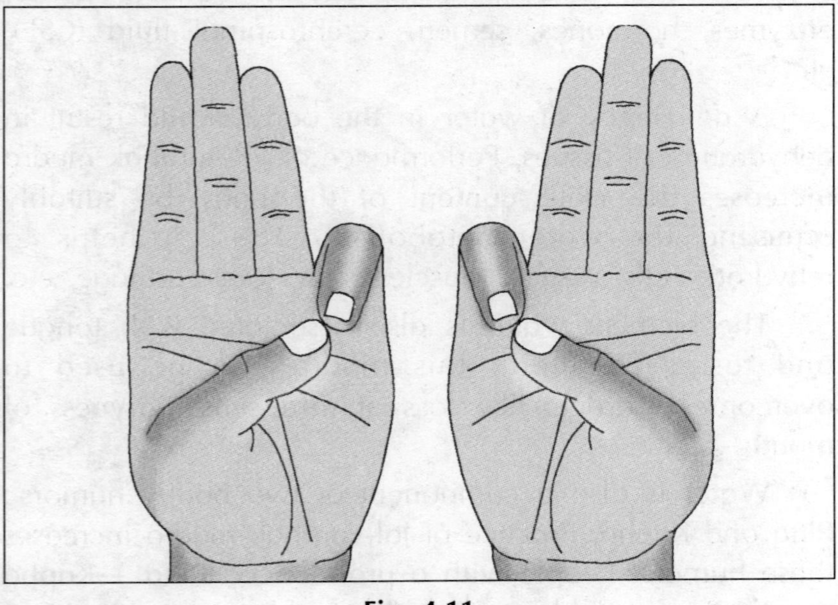

Fig. 4.11

Effects : Jal-vardhak (Varun) mudra increases the Jal (water) element within the body.

Almost seventy per cent of the body is water. Thus, water is the most abundant element in the body, being present in the protoplasm of cells, extra-cellular fluid, lymph, blood, tears, saliva, mucous, digestive juices, enzymes, hormones, semen, cerebrospinal fluid (CSF), etc.

A deficiency of water in the body would result in dehydration of tissues. Performance of Jal-vardhak mudra increases the water-content of the body by suitably affecting the water-metabolism. Thus, it helps to rehydrate cells, tissues, muscles, skin, joint-cartilage, etc.

The element water is also associated with tongue and taste. Therefore, this mudra can be used to overcome disorders like loss of taste-sense, dryness of mouth, etc.

Water is also a component of two bodily humors : Pitta and Kapha. Practice of Jal-vardhak mudra increases these humors. People with a pronounced Pitta + Kapha constitution should perform this mudra in moderation. On the other hand, people with a Vaata constitution (dosha) can derive immense benefits from the practice of this mudra.

Benefits : Jal-vardhak (Varun) mudra can be used to overcome the following disorders :

(1) Dryness of eyes,

(2) Dryness of the digestive tract (mouth, throat and intestines),

(3) Indigestion,

(4) Constipation,

(5) Dryness of the skin leading to cracks, dry eczema, psoriasis, etc.,

(6) Degeneration of joint-cartilage, Osteo-Arthritis,

(7) Anaemia,

(8) Cramps, dehydration,

(9) Deficiency of hormones,

(10) Scanty urination (oliguria),

(11) Scanty semen (oligospermia),

(12) Scanty menses (oligomenorrhoea),

(13) Loss of taste sensation, tongue-disorders,

(14) Disorders of Vaata-excess (see Vaayu-shaamak mudra).

Duration : 45 minutes every day, either at one stretch or in 3 parts (i.e., for 15 minutes, thrice a day).

Ideal time : None

Precaution : People having water-retention in their bodies or people with a Pitta + Kapha constitution should perform this mudra moderately, if at all.

(8) Jal-shaamak (जल-शामक) mudra

Jal-shaamak mudra brings about a reduction of the Jal (water) element within the body.

Method : This mudra is formed by first placing the tip of the little finger on the base of the thumb and then bringing gentle pressure of the thumb upon this finger. This amounts to suppression of element water (residing in the little finger) by element fire (residing in the thumb).

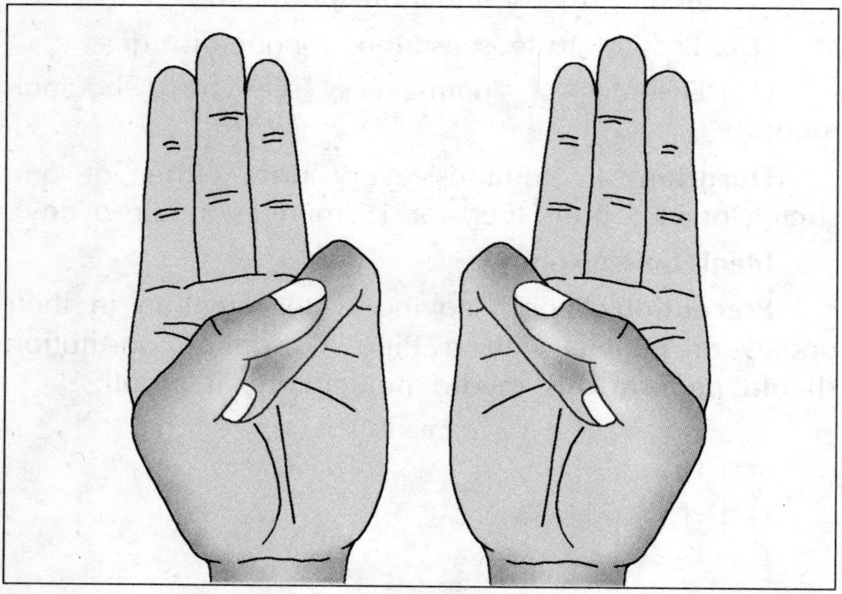

Fig. 4.12

Effects : Jal-shaamak mudra reduces the water-content of the body by suitably affecting the water-metabolism. It can, therefore, be used to overcome water-logging within the body.

Water is also a component of the two bodily humors : Pitta and Kapha. Practice of Jal-shaamak mudra brings about a reduction of these humors. People with a pronounced Pitta + Kapha constitution can immensely benefit by the practice of this mudra. Such people can regularly practise this mudra even to prevent illness.

Benefits : Jal-shaamak mudra can be used to overcome the following disorders :

(1) Oedema (water-retention),

(2) Ascitis, dropsy,

(3) Excessive salivation,

(4) Watery eyes,

(5) Running nose,

(6) Hyperacidity,

(7) Diarrhoea (loose motions),

(8) Pleural effusion (pleurisy),

(9) Effusion in a joint,

(10) Excess of hormones,

(11) Excessive menses (menorrhagia),

(12) Hydrocele,

(13) Hydrocephalous,

(14) Hydronephrosis,

(15) Cold and clamy body / hands / feet,

(16) Disorders of Vaata deficiency (see Vaayu-vardhak mudra).

Duration : 45 minutes every day, either at one stretch or in 3 parts (i.e., for 15 minutes, thrice a day).

Ideal time : None

Precautions : Experienced doctors say that the practice of this mudra should be discontinued as soon as the disease has been overcome.

(9) Vaata-kaarak (वात-कारक) or Vaayan mudra

Also called **Vaata** or **Vaayan mudra**, this mudra increases the **Vaata humor** within the body.

Method : This mudra is formed by joining together the tips of the thumb, the index finger and the middle finger.

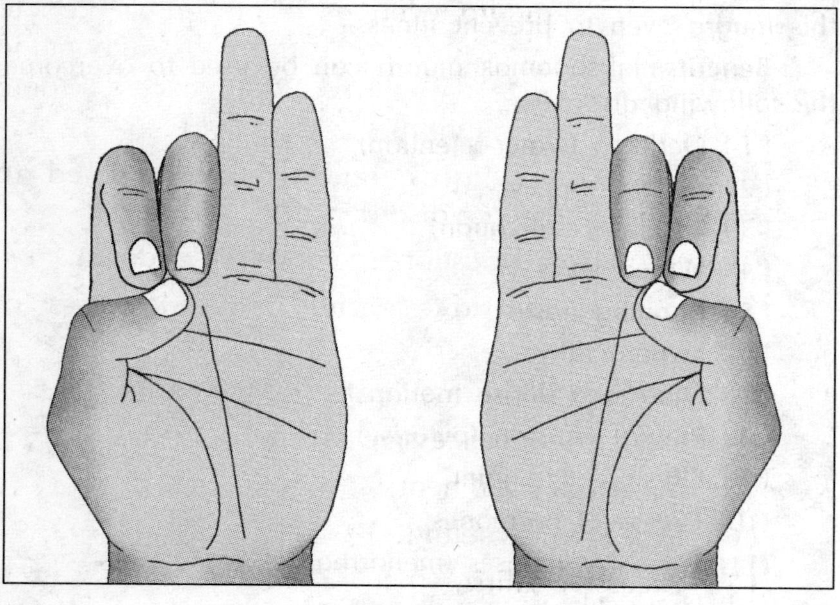

Fig. 4.13

Effects : The **Vaata humor** controls the nervous system which, in turn, is responsible for various bodily movements : external as well as internal. Practice of **Vaata-kaarak mudra** increases the **Vaata humor** within the body, thereby boosting the nerve force and the vital power. In other words, this is an excellent mudra for people having a Vaata deficiency. In fact, such people can practise this mudra even as a preventive i.e., to avert illness. However, this mudra should be done in moderation by people who have Vaata excess (Vaata dosha or Vaata constitution).

Benefits : Vaata-kaarak mudra can be used to overcome the following disorders :

(1) Nervous exhaustion, nervous breakdown,

(2) Lack of initiave/enthusiasm, slowness of thoughts/perception,

(3) Lethargy, laziness, general debility,

(4) Drowsiness, excessive sleep,

(5) Intolerance of heat; sunstroke,

(6) Excessive sweating,

(7) Excessive thirst,

(8) Frequent, profuse urination,

(9) Loss of appetite,

(10) Fatness,

(11) Loose motions,

(12) Menorrhagia (excessive menstrual bleeding),

(13) Greasy skin, hair,

(14) Disorders caused by a deficiency of air element within the body (see Vaayu-vardhak mudra).

Duration : 45 minutes every day, either at one stretch or in 3 parts (i.e., 15 minutes, thrice a day).

Ideal time : Though Vaata-kaarak mudra can be performed at anytime of the day, practising it at anytime from 2.00 to 6.00 am/pm gives better results.

Precaution : People with a pronounced Vaata constitution should perform this mudra in moderation, if at all.

Note : A person desirous of enhancing or boosting the effects of **Vaata-kaarak mudra** can combine it with **Kapha-naashak mudra**

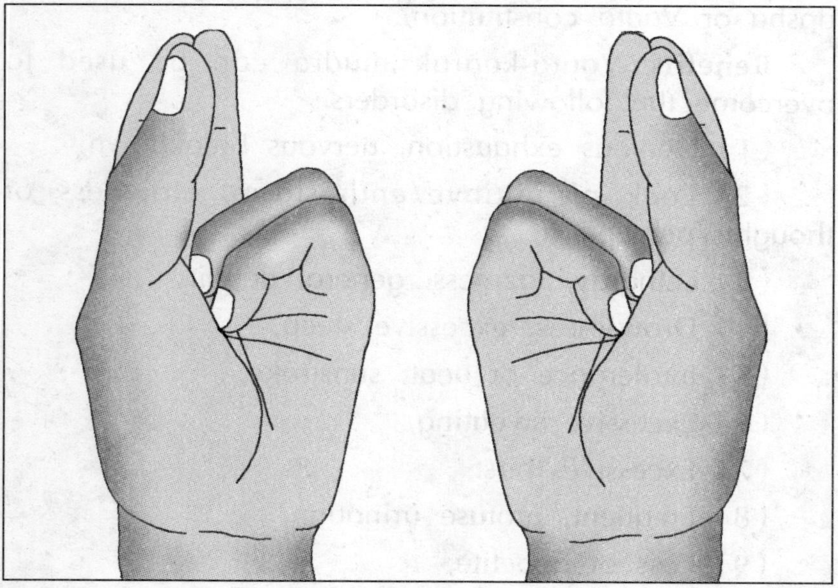

Fig. 4.14

Some variations of Vaata-kaarak mudra

Given below are some variations of **Vaata-kaarak mudra** which, apart from giving the benefits already mentioned, bestows some additional gains.

(a) Udaan (उदान) mudra

This mudra benefits the vocal cords (voice), the respiratory system and the thyroid-parathyroid glands.

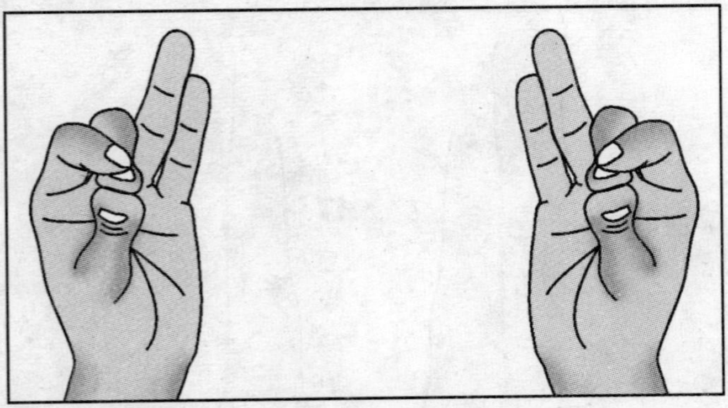

Fig. 4.15

(b) Vyaan (व्यान) mudra

This mudra is useful for ailments of the heart and the blood-circulatory system.

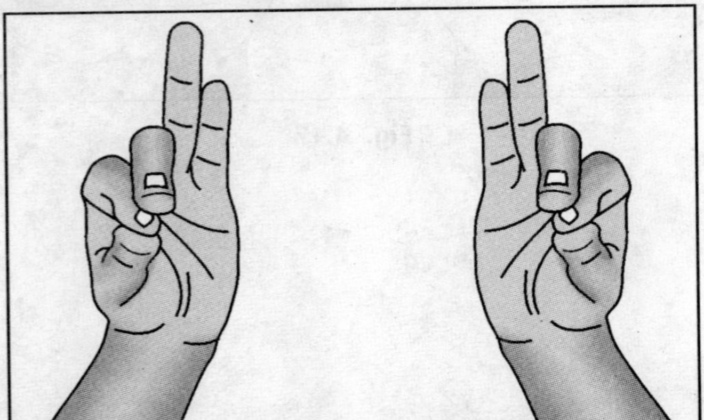

Fig. 4.16

(10) Vaata-naashak (वात-नाशक) mudra

The **Vaata-naashak mudra** brings about a reduction of the **Vaata humor** within the body.

Method : This mudra is formed by first placing the tips of the index and the middle fingers on the base of the thumb and then bringing gentle pressure of the thumb upon these fingers.

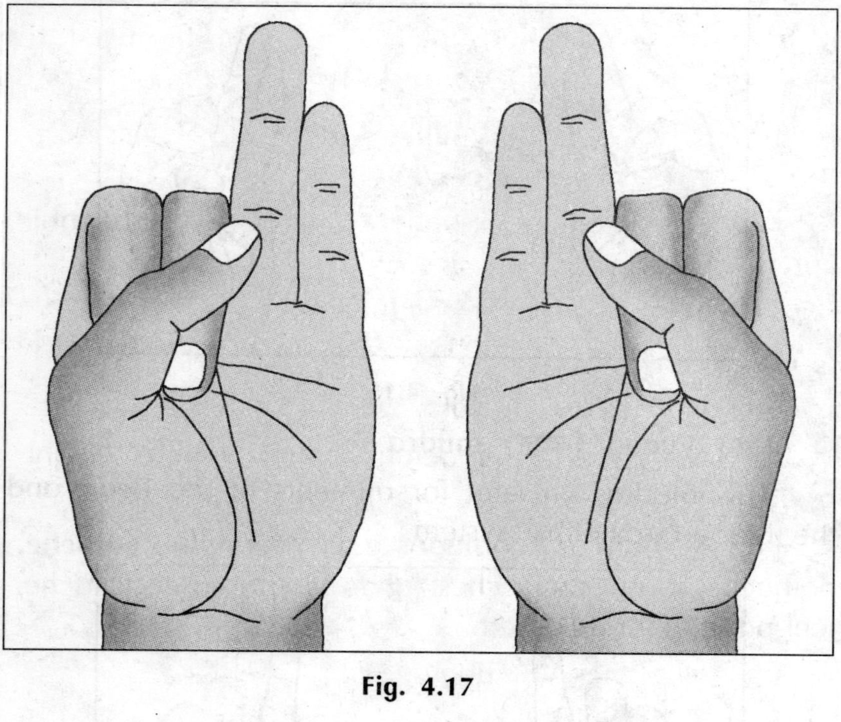

Fig. 4.17

Effects : Practice of **Vaata-naashak mudra** pacifies the aggravated **Vaata humor**. It is, therefore, an excellent mudra for people with a pronounced **Vaata constitution (Vaata dosha)**. In fact, they can regularly perform this mudra even to avoid illness. However, people who already have a deficiency of Vaata (e.g., people suffering from paralysis) should practise this mudra in moderation, if at all.

Benefits : Vaata-naashak mudra can be used to overcome the following disorders :

(1) Chronic/easy fatigue,

(2) Lack of stamina/endurance,

(3) Indecisiveness, impatience, timidity, inexplicable fear, etc.,

(4) Poor memory, forgetfulness,

(5) Sleeplessness,

(6) Intolerance of cold weather/wind,

(7) Underweight, emaciation, inexplicable weight-loss,

(8) All painful conditions e.g., headache, earache, toothache, throat pain, chest/abdominal pain, backache, heel-pain, joint-pain, etc.,

(9) Numbness in body-parts,

(10) Tremors, shivering,

(11) Unsteady gait (walk), Parkinsonism, giddiness, vertigo,

(12) Creaking joints, Osteo-Arthritis,

(13) Cold, dry, cracked skin, nails, hair,

(14) Irregular, scanty, painful menses,

(15) Hoarseness of voice, stammering,

(16) Constipation, flatulence (gas),

(17) Scanty urination (oliguria),

(18) Scanty sweating,

(19) Disorders caused by an excess of air element within the body (see Vaayu-shaamak mudra).

Duration : 45 minutes every day, either at one stretch or in three parts (i.e., for 15 minutes, thrice a day).

Ideal time : Though Vaata-naashak mudra can be performed at anytime of the day, practising it at anytime other than 2.00 to 6.00 am/pm gives better results.

Note : A person desirous of enhancing or boosting the effects of **Vaata-naashak mudra** can combine it with **Kapha-kaarak mudra.**

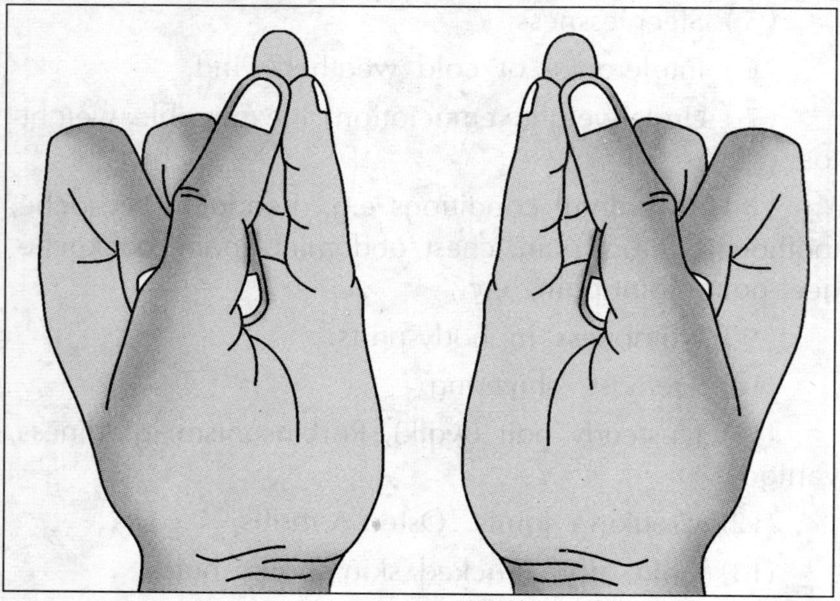

Fig. 4.18

(11) Pitta-kaarak (पित्त-कारक) or Kapha-naashak (कफ-नाशक) mudra

The **Pitta-kaarak** mudra brings about an increase in the **Pitta humor** within the body. At the same time, it effects a reduction in the **Kapha humor** within the body. It can, therefore, also be called **kapha-naashak mudra**.

Method : This mudra is formed by first placing the ring and the little fingers on the base of the thumb and then bringing gentle pressure of the thumb upon these fingers.

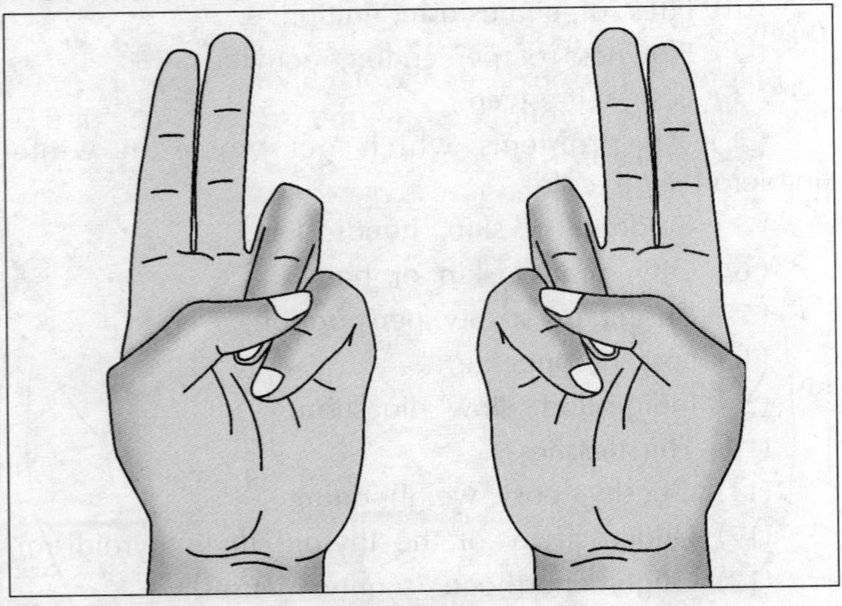

Fig. 4.19

Effects : This mudra increases the **Pitta humor** but decreases the **Kapha humor** within the body. Pitta is concerned with the bodily heat (digestion/metabolism) and the circulatory system. These entities are stimulated and reinforced by this mudra. This is an excellent mudra for people having a kapha-excess or a Pitta-deficiency in their bodies. They can regularly perform this mudra even to prevent illness. However, people who have an excess of Pitta (heat) in their bodies should practise it in moderation, if at all.

Benefits : Pitta-kaarak (kapha-naashak) mudra can be practised to overcome the following disorders :

(1) Lack of enthusiasm, initiative,

(2) Slowness of perception, activities,

(3) Low self-esteem,

(4) All problems which get worse in winter (intolerance of cold),

(5) Coldness of skin, hands, feet,

(6) Oily, greasy skin or hair,

(7) Absent or scanty perspiration,

(8) Loss of appetite,

(9) Indigestion, slow digestion,

(10) Thirstlessness,

(11) Obesity, easy weight-gain,

(12) Underactivity of the thyroid (hypothyroidism),

(13) Oligomenorrhoea (scanty menses),

(14) Excessive mucous in the respiratory / digestive tracts causing colds, wet cough, sticky stools, etc.,

(15) Eye ailments like watering, stickiness, etc.,

(16) Disorders caused by an excess of earth and water elements within the body [see Prithvi-shaamak (Surya) and Jal-shaamak mudras].

Duration : 45 minutes every day, either at one stretch, or in 3 parts (i.e., for 15 minutes, thrice a day).

Ideal time : Though Pitta-kaarak mudra can be performed at anytime of the day, practising it anytime from 10 am to 2 pm/am gives better results.

Precaution : A person having a pronounced Pitta constitution should perform this mudra in moderation, if at all.

Note : A person desirous of enhancing or boosting the effects of **Pitta-kaarak mudra** can combine it with **Vaata-naashak mudra.**

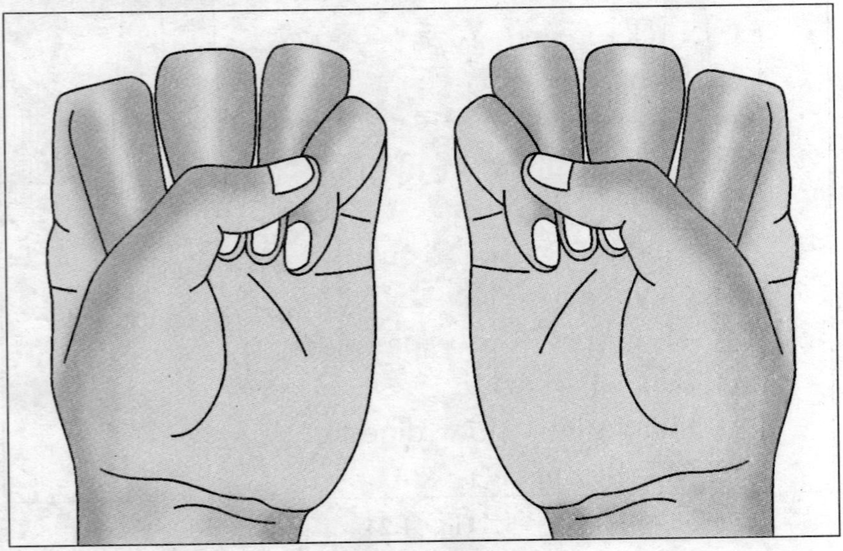

Fig. 4.20

(12) Kapha-kaarak (कफ-कारक) or Pitta-naashak (पित्त-नाशक) mudra

Popularly known as **Praan mudra**, this mudra increases the **Kapha humor** but decreases the **Pitta humor** within the body.

Method : This mudra is formed by joining together the tips of the thumb, the ring finger and the little finger.

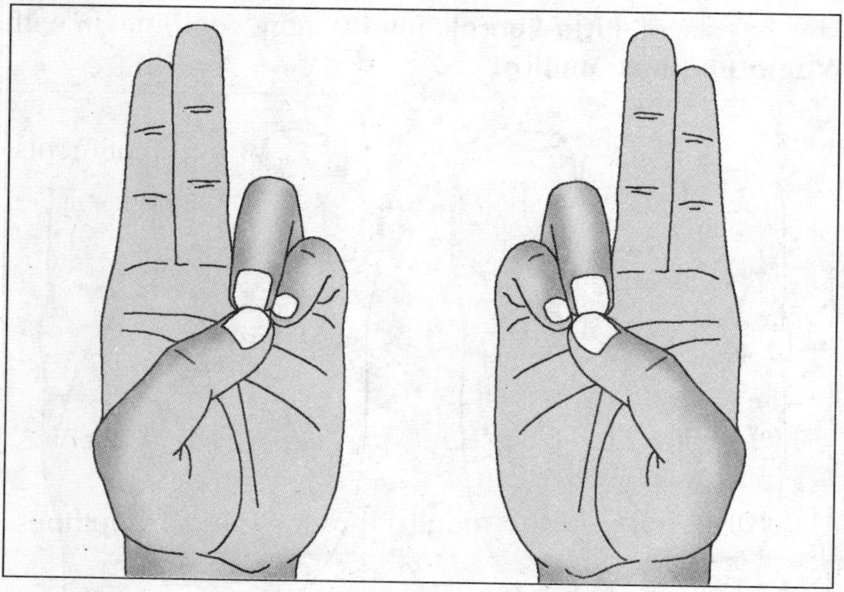

Fig. 4.21

Effects : This mudra brings about an increase of **Kapha humor** within the body. **Kapha humor** is associated with vitality, strength and immunity. Practice of **Praan mudra** increases these qualities. This mudra also reduces **Pitta humor**, which is associated with bodily heat and metabolism. Thus, this mudra is excellent for people who have an excess of Pitta or a deficiency of kapha in their bodies. They can regularly perform this mudra even to avert illness. On the other hand, people with a kapha-excess or Pitta-deficiency should perform this mudra in moderation, if at all.

Benefits : Kapha-kaarak (Pitta-naashak) or Praan mudra can be used to overcome the following disorders :

(1) Chronic fatigue, general debility, low endurance,

(2) Impaired immunity (tendency to contract infectious diseases),

(3) Mental tension, anger, irritability, jealousness, pride, impatience, chronic sense of time-urgency,

(4) Forgetfulness,

(5) Intolerance of heat, stress and noise; ailments which get worse in summer,

(6) Hyperthyroidism (weight-loss despite having good appetite),

(7) Inflammatory disorders (diseases ending with 'itis'),

(8) Sleeplessness; light/disturbed sleep,

(9) High blood pressure, athero-sclerosis (hardening and narrowing of arteries),

(10) Burning in the mouth, throat, stomach; apthous ulcers, acidity, ulcerative colitis,

(11) Loose, bloody stools; dysentery,

(12) Scanty, burning urination,

(13) Excessive, foul-smelling perspiration,

(14) Excessive, painful menses,

(15) Red-hot joints; Rheumatoid Arthritis; instability of joints,

(16) Burning, red, dry eyes; Cataract,

(17) Dry, red, hot, ageing, skin; skin-rashes; urticaria, leprosy,

(18) Dry, sparse, grey hair,

(19) Jaundice,

(20) Premature ageing,

(21) Disorders caused by a deficiency of earth and water elements within the body [see **Prithvi-vardhak** and **Jal-vardhak (varun) mudras**].

Duration : Weak, debilitated, immunity-compromised people should practise this mudra for a **minimum** of 45 minutes every day, either at one stretch or in three parts (i.e., for 15 minutes, thrice a day).

Ideal time : Though this mudra can be performed anytime, practising it between 6.00 to 10.00 am/pm gives better results.

Precaution : People who are overweight or who have a pronounced kapha constitution should perform this mudra in moderation, if at all.

Note : A person desirous of boosting or enhancing the effects of **Kapha-kaarak (Pitta-naashak) mudra** should combine it with **Vaata-naashak mudra.**

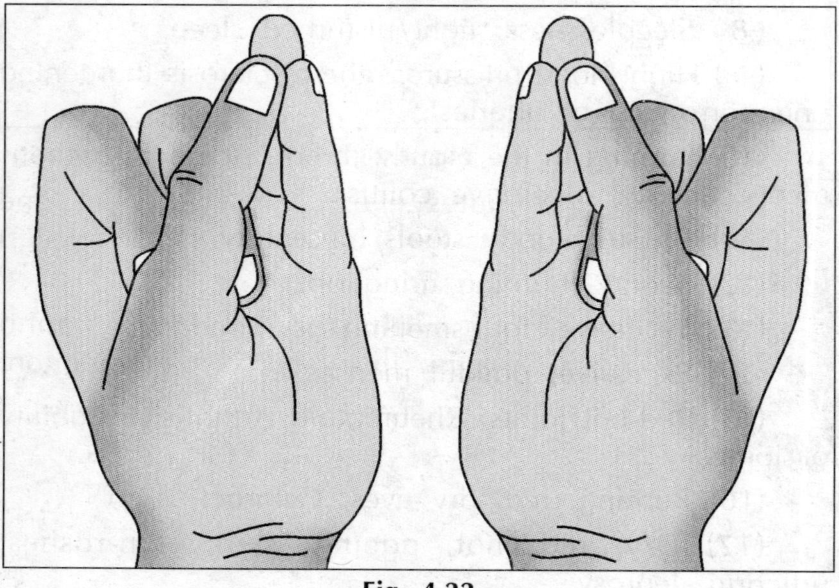

Fig. 4.22

(13) (Vaata + Pitta)-naashak (वातपित्त-नाशक) mudra

This mudra helps to overcome any ailment of a person having a **Vaata + Pitta mix constitution.**

Method : This mudra is formed by (1) placing the index finger on the base of the thumb and (2) joining together the tips of the thumb and the ring finger.

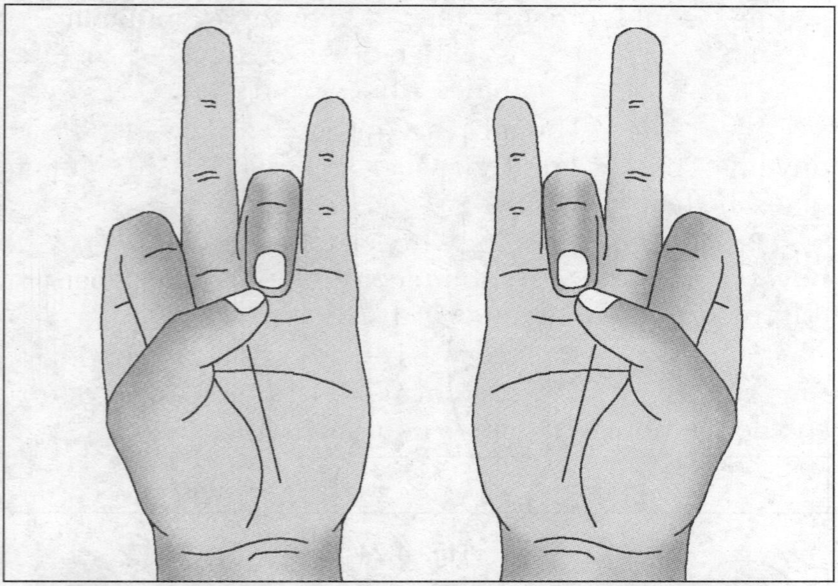

Fig. 4.23

Duration : 45 minutes every day, either at one stretch or in three parts (i.e., for 15 minutes, thrice a day).

Precaution : People with a pronounced kapha constitution should practise this mudra in moderation, if at all.

(14) (Vaata + Kapha)-naashak (वातकफ-नाशक) mudra

This mudra helps to overcome any ailment of a person having a **Vaata + Kapha mix constitution.**

Method : This mudra is formed by applying the tips of the index and the ring fingers to the base of the thumb.

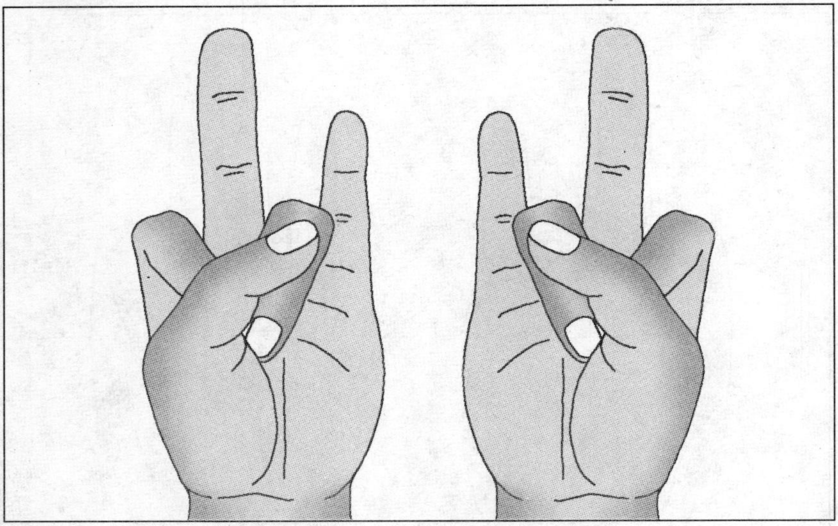

Fig. 4.24

Duration : 45 minutes every day, either at one stretch or in three parts (i.e., for 15 minutes, thrice a day).

Precaution : People with a pronounced Pitta constitution should practise this mudra in moderation, if at all.

(15) (Pitta + Kapha)-naashak (पित्तकफ-नाशक) mudra

This mudra helps to overcome any ailment of a person having a **Pitta + Kapha mix constitution.**

Method : This mudra is formed by (1) joining together the tips of the thumb and the ring finger and (2) applying the tip of the little finger to the base of the thumb.

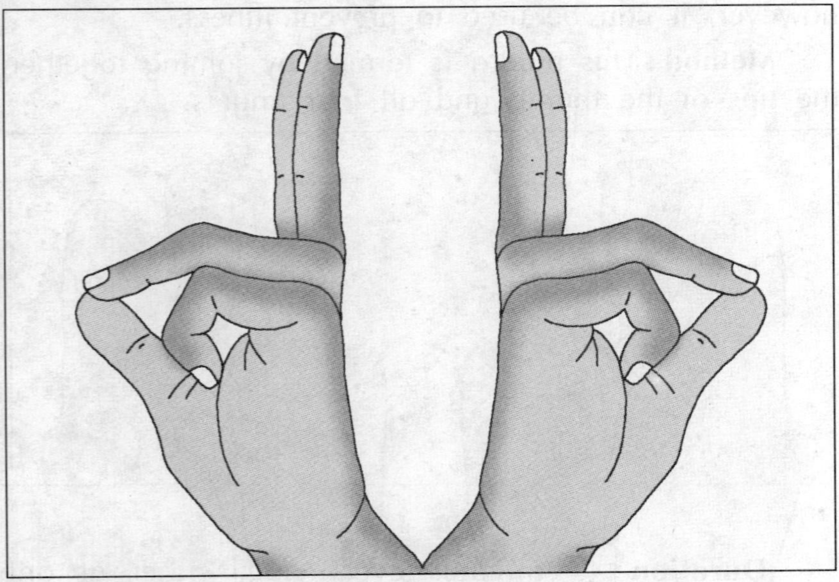

Fig. 4.25

Duration : 45 minutes every day, either at one stretch or in three parts (i.e., for 15 minutes, thrice a day).

Precaution : People with a pronounced Vaata constitution should practise this mudra in moderation, if at all.

(16) Tridosha-naashak 'Samaan' (समान) mudra

At times also called the **Mukul mudra** or the **Sukri mudra**, this mudra balances and co-ordinates the five elements and the three humors of the body. Therefore, this mudra is useful for a person, whose all three humors have become deranged. Theoretically, this mudra can be used to overcome any disorder. More importantly, however, it can be used to prevent illness.

Method : This mudra is formed by joining together the tips of the thumb and all four fingers.

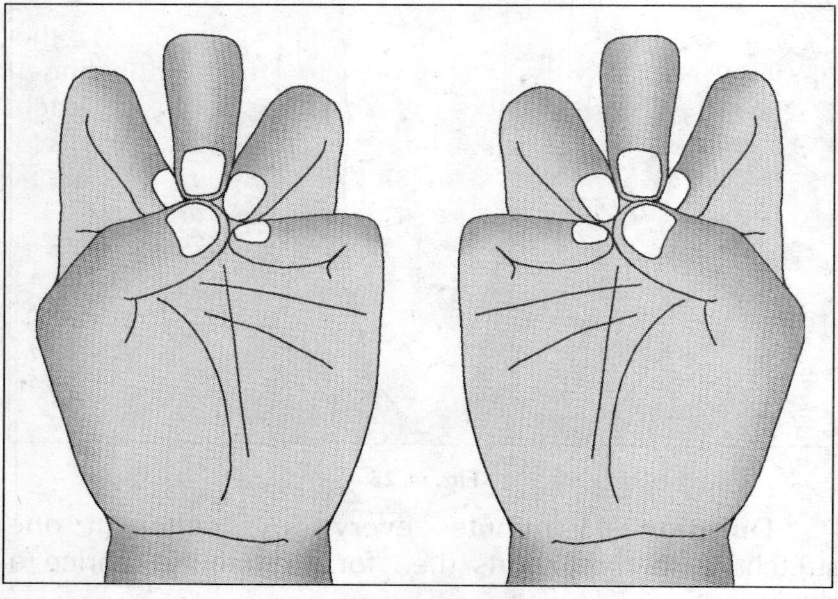

Fig. 4.26

Duration : 45 minutes every day, either at one stretch or in three parts (i.e., for 15 minutes, thrice a day).

Precaution : None

Note : While performing this mudra, the fingertips can be directed at (or touched to) the diseased part of the body.

(17) Tridosha-naashak 'Surabhi' (सुरभि) mudra

Also known as the **Kaamadhenu mudra**, this mudra balances and co-ordinates the five elements and the three humors of the body. While the effects of this mudra are similar to those of the Samaan mudra, it is much more difficult to perform.

Surabhi means a cow. In fact, **Kaamadhenu** is a mythological, heavenly cow which is believed to fulfill all wishes. By regularly performing this mudra, the practitioner can succeed in realizing all his dreams and fulfilling all his wishes !

Method : This mudra is formed by joining (1) the tip of ring finger of each hand to the tip of little finger of the other and (2) the tip of index finger of each hand to the tip of middle finger of the other. The two thumbs lie side by side, touching each other. This forms a figure that resembles the four udders of a cow.

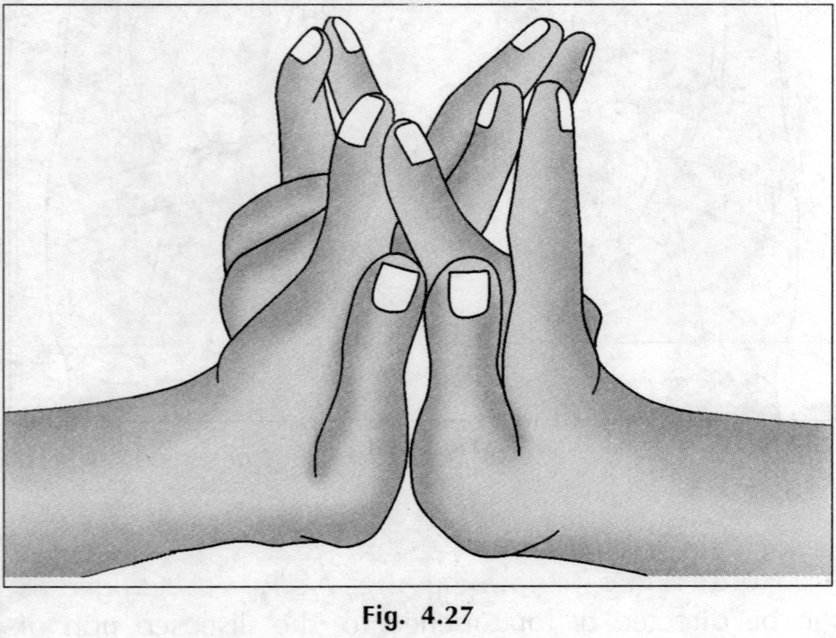

Fig. 4.27

Duration : 45 minutes every day, either at one stretch or in three parts (i.e., for 15 minutes, thrice a day).

Precaution : None

(18) Apaan (अपान) mudra

The Apaan mudra is an extremely important and useful mudra that first detoxifies (and, therefore, purifies) the body and then energizes it.

Method : Apaan mudra is formed by joining together the tips of the thumb, the middle finger and the ring finger.

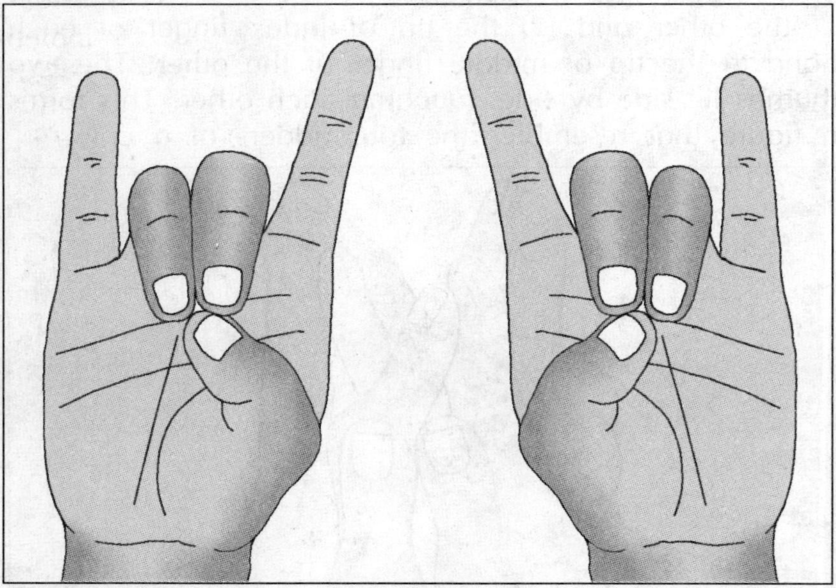

Fig. 4.28

Effects : Apaan mudra is a combination of the **Aakaash-vardhak (Aakaash)** and the **Prithvi-vardhak (Prithvi) mudras.** Apart from an increase of elements space and earth, Apaan mudra brings about an increase of **Vaata** and **Kapha humors** and, therefore, a decrease of **Pitta humor.**

Benefits : The Apaan mudra can be used to overcome the following disorders :

(1) Anuria (absence/obstruction of urine),

(2) Constipation, flatulence (gas), piles,

(3) Absence of sweat,

(4) Delayed delivery of a child,

(5) Burning in the body / body-parts,

(6) Ailments caused by a deficiency of element space and humor Vaata,

(7) Ailments caused by a deficiency of element earth and humor Kapha,

(8) Ailments caused by an excess of element fire and humor Pitta.

Duration : Minimum 45 minutes every day, either at one stretch or in three parts (i.e., for 15 minutes, thrice a day).

Precaution : People with a Vaata + Kapha mix constitution should perform this mudra in moderation.

(19) Apaan-vaayu (अपान-वायु) mudra

This important mudra is sometimes called **'Mrit-sanjeevani' mudra,** a mudra which can snatch a person away from the clutches of death ! Indeed, this mudra tremendously benefits a person who has suffered from chest-pain (angina pectoris) or a heart-attack. It increases the **earth** element (and, therefore, the **Kapha** humor) while decreasing the **air** and **fire** elements within the body.

Method : This mudra is formed by (1) joining together the tips of thumb, middle and ring fingers and (2) applying the tip of index finger to the base of the thumb.

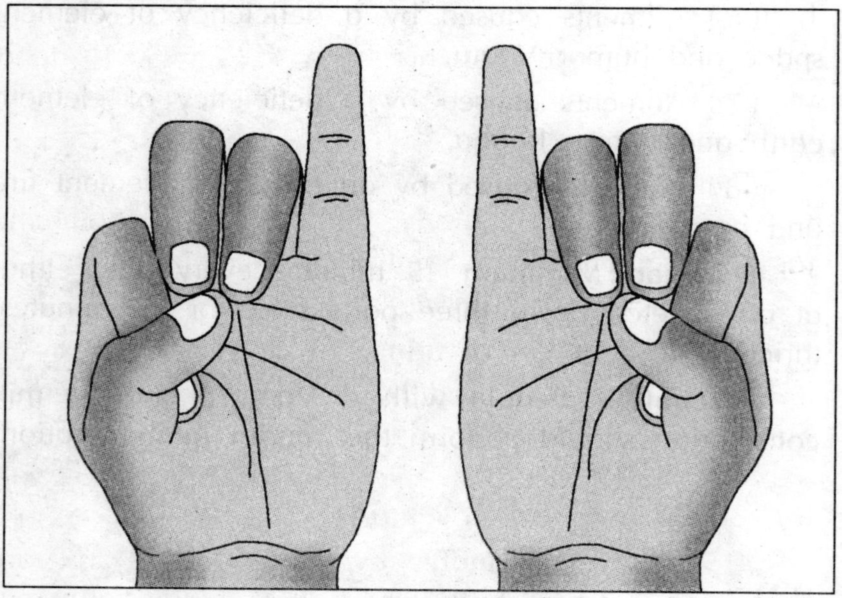

Fig. 4.29

Effects : This mudra bestows triple benefits :

(1) Removal of obstructions/blockages in, and detoxification of, the body to allow an increase of element Aakaash (space),

(2) Increase of vitality due to an increase of element Prithvi (earth) and

(3) Sedation of the mind and relaxation of the body/muscles due to a reduction of element Vaayu (air).

Benefits : Apaan-vaayu mudra can be used to overcome the following disorders :

(1) Fast heart beats, palpitations,

(2) Angina pectoris (chest pain caused by blockages within the coronary arteries that nourish the heart),

(3) Performance of this mudra as soon as a heart-attack strikes might enable the victim to minimize damage to the heart-muscle,

(4) High blood pressure,

(5) Painful conditions like headache, toothache, tummyache, backache, joint-pains, heel pain, etc.,

(6) Excessive sweating,

(7) Obstruction of urine,

(8) Ailments caused by a deficiency of element earth or humor kapha,

(9) Ailments caused by an excess of elements air, fire and humors Vaata, Pitta.

Duration : 45 minutes every day, either at one stretch or in three parts (i.e., for 15 minutes, thrice a day). However, when suffering from chest-pain, it should be performed continuously till the pain subsides.

Precaution : People having a pronounced kapha constitution should perform this mudra in moderation.

(20) Linga (लिंग) mudra

Linga is the Sanskrit term for phallus (the male genital organ). This mudra increases bodily heat since it reinforces the **fire** element and the **Pitta** humor.

Method : This mudra is formed by interlocking the palms but keeping the left thumb erect, pointing upwards.

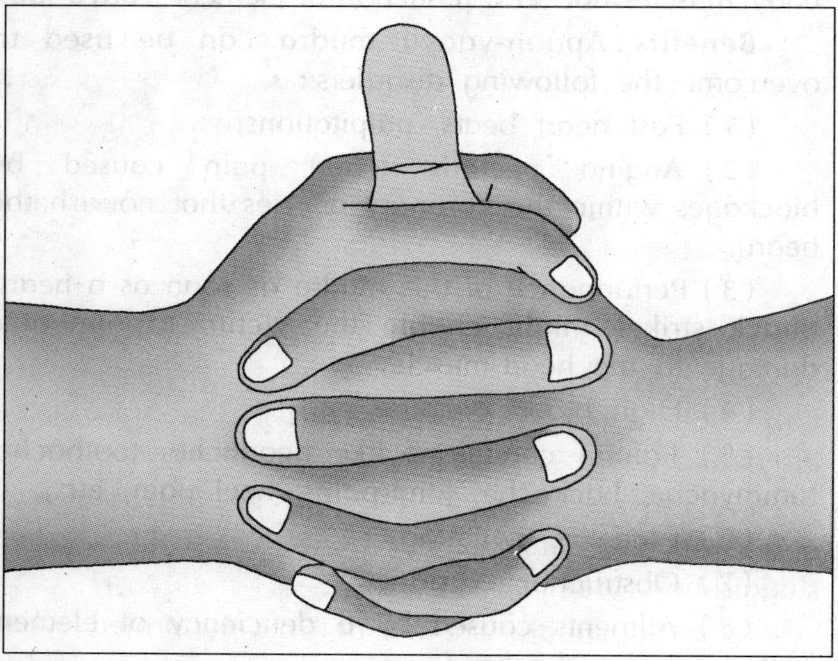

Fig. 4.30

Effects : The thumb represents the element **fire**. This fire is reinforced by performing the linga mudra. The **fire** element which resides in the thumb is activated and is able to increase uninhibited.

Benefits : The linga mudra can be used to overcome the following disorders :

(1) Shivering and chills due to intolerance of cold weather; hypothermia,

(2) Ailments caused by an overproduction/ accumulation of phlegm (mucous) in the body; such ailments include colds, sinusitis, productive (wet) cough, sticky stools, etc.,

(3) Asthma and other respiratory ailments that occur at the change of weather,

(4) Sexual debility in males.

Duration : This mudra is not to be performed on a regular basis. It should be performed only when needed (e.g., when suffering from chills) and should be discontinued once the ailment has been overcome.

Precautions : (1) Overuse of Linga mudra may aggravate the Pitta humor within the body, causing sluggishness and lethargy.

(2) This mudra should not be performed when suffering from ailments of Pitta-excess, especially fever.

(21) Shankha (शंख) mudra

Shankha is the Indian term for a conch. When this mudra is performed, the hands resemble a conch.

Method : First, clench the left thumb with right fingers. Now, place the left fingers on the back of the right palm. Finally, join the tips of the right thumb and the left index finger.

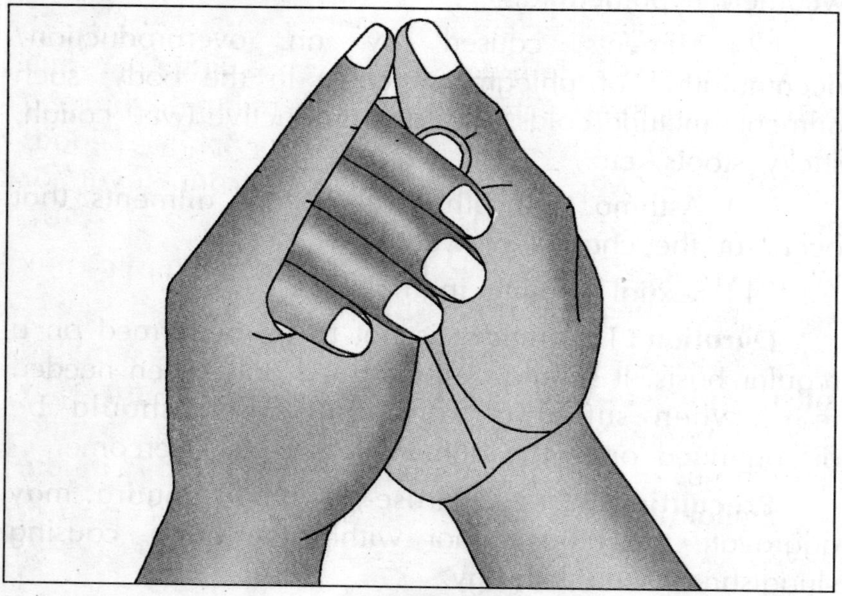

Fig. 4.31

Effects : The thumb, which represents the element **fire,** is encircled (and thereby subdued) by the fingers. At the same time, the union of left index finger and the right thumb results in an increase of element **air**. In other words, the **Shankha mudra** brings about a decrease of **Pitta humor** but an increase of **Vaata and kapha humors** within the body.

Benefits : Shankha mudra can be used to overcome the following disorders :

(1) Feverish feeling in the body,

(2) Burning in the body/body-parts,

(3) Allergic disorders, especially urticaria (skin-rashes),

(4) Voice (larynx) and throat (pharynx) problems,

(5) Flabbiness / weakness / paralysis of muscles.

Duration : 45 minutes every day, either at one stretch or in three parts (i.e., for 15 minutes, thrice a day). However, it may be performed for longer periods if necessary (e.g.; when suffering from fever or manifestations of allergy).

Precaution : People with a Vaata + kapha mix constitution should perform this mudra in moderation.

Note : There is a simplified version of this mudra called **'Sahaj shankha mudra'**, which is performed by interlocking the eight fingers and bringing in contact the two upward-pointing thumbs. Benefits of this mudra are similar to those of the **Shankha mudra.**

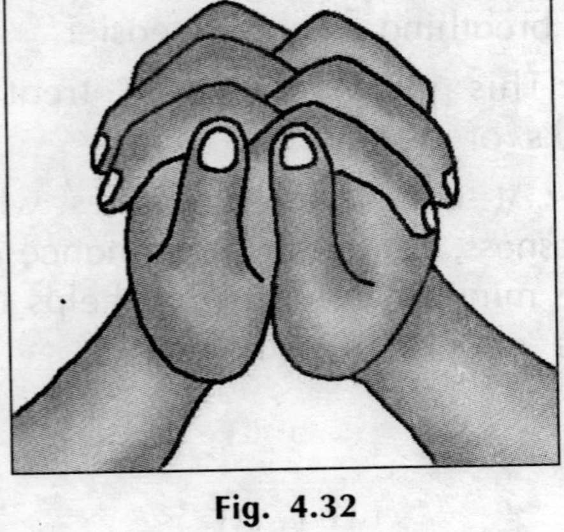

Fig. 4.32

(22) Asthma mudra

Like Aakaash-vardhak [or Aakaash], Prithvi-shaamak [or Surya] and Linga mudras, this mudra too can help asthmatics, enabling them to relieve an attack of asthma.

Method : Press together the finger-nails of the middle fingers, keeping the other fingers gently extended.

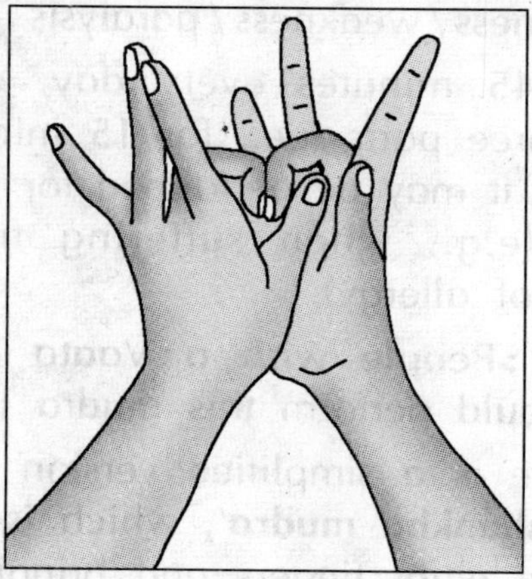

Fig. 4.33

Effects : This mudra relaxes the smoothe muscles that line the respiratory tract. With the bronchial spasm thus relieved, the breathing becomes easier.

Benefits : This mudra helps to treat as well as prevent attacks of asthma.

Duration : At least fifteen minutes when suffering from breathlessness. A regular performance of this mudra for about five minutes thrice a day helps the person to prevent future attacks of asthma.

(23) Maatangi mudra

Maatangi is the God of inner harmony. Performance of this mudra enables a person to attain harmony with himself and with the surroundings.

Method : Interlock the hands (held at navel level), keeping the middle fingers straight and touching each other.

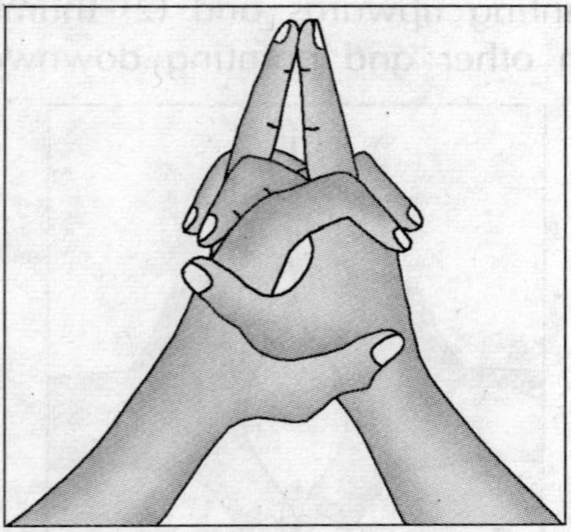

Fig. 4.34

Effects : This mudra beneficially affects the hypothalamus which is a part of the brain.

Benefits : Since hypothalamus is the seat of autonomous nervous system, this mudra establishes a state of balance (i.e., homoeostasis) within the body. It also relieves tension and pain in organs of the chest and the abdomen.

Duration : (1) For at least fifteen minutes when suffering from internal pain.

(2) For five minutes, thrice a day to attain and maintain internal harmony.

(24) Uttarabodhi mudra

Uttarabodhi mudra can be called the mudra of enlightenment. And as the sun of enlightenment dawns, fears are dispelled. Thus this mudra works like (and, therefore, can complement) Abhay-gyaan mudra.

Method : Interlock the hands (held at navel level), keeping the (1) index fingers straight, touching each other and pointing upwards and (2) thumbs extended, touching each other and pointing downwards.

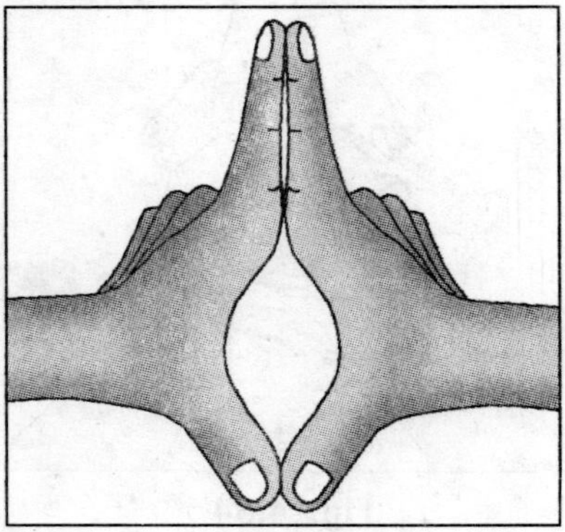

Fig. 4.35

Effects : A regular practice of this mudra brings about a realisation that we should fear nothing or nobody except God.

Benefits : (1) Helps to soothe excited nerves before beginning a daunting task.

(2) Enables the performer to overcome examination-nerves, stage-fright, etc.

Duration : For fifteen minutes or more, as and when required.

(25) Pushaan mudra

This mudra is dedicated to Pushaan or sun, the God of warmth, energy and nourishment.

Method : With the right hand, perform the Vaata-kaarak mudra and with the left hand, perform the Apaan mudra.

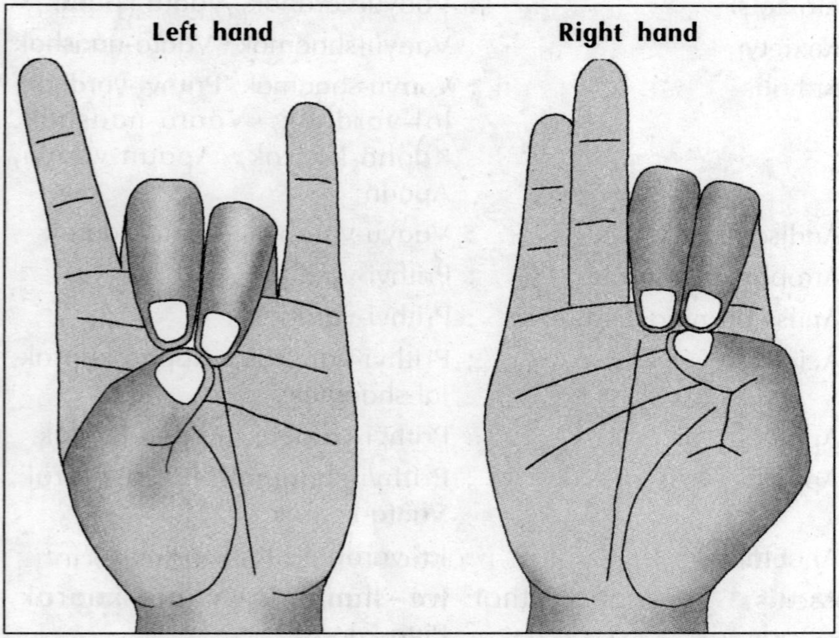

Fig. 4.36

Effects : Pushaan mudra increases the space, the air, and the earth elements of the body.

Benefits : (1) Increases energy and immunity.

(2) Increases strength, stamina and endurance.

(3) Detoxifies the body by facilitating excretion of metabolic waste products through stools, urine and sweat.

Duration : For 45 minutes every day, either at one stretch or in three parts, of 15 minutes each.

SECTION III

5. THERAPEUTIC INDEX

Ⓐ

Alzheimer's disease	: Vaayu-vardhak, Vaata-kaarak
Ataxia(s)	: Vaayu-vardhak, Vaata-kaarak
Anxiety	: Vaayu-shaamak, Vaata-naashak
Arthritis	: Vaayu-shaamak, Prithvi-vardhak, Jal-vardhak, Vaata-naashak, Kapha-kaarak, Apaan-vaayu, Apaan
Addison's disease	: Vaayu-vardhak, Vaata-kaarak
Atrophy of muscles	: Prithvi-vardhak
Anus, burning/fissure in	: Prithvi-vardhak
Acidity	: Prithvi-vardhak, Kapha-kaarak, Jal-shaamak
Aphthous ulcers	: Prithvi-vardhak, Kapha-kaarak
Appetite, loss of	: Prithvi-shaamak, Pitta-kaarak, Vaata-kaarak
Anaemia	: Jal-vardhak, Kapha-kaarak
Ascitis	: Jal-shaamak, Vaata-kaarak, Pitta-kaarak
Abdominal pain	: Vaata-naashak, Vaayu-shaamak, Apaan-vayu, Maatangi
Anger	: Kapha-kaarak, Prithvi-vardhak, Vaayu-shaamak
Athero-sclerosis	: Kapha-kaarak
Ageing, premature	: Prithvi-vardhak, Kapha-kaarak
Acne	: Vaayu-vardhak
Anuria	: Apaan, Apaan-vaayu, Jal-vardhak

Angina pectoris	: Apaan-vaayu, Aakaash-vardhak
Asthma	: Linga, Prithvi-shaamak, Aakaash-vardhak, Asthma
Allergy	: Shankha, Prithvi-vardhak, Kapha-kaarak
Appendicitis	: Prithvi-vardhak, Apaan-vaayu
Atrophy of optic nerve	: Prithvi-vardhak, Vaayu-vardhak

(B)

Bradycardia	: Vaayu-vardhak
Breathlessness	: Vaayu-shaamak, Asthma
Brittle nails	: Vaayu-shaamak, Prithvi-vardhak
Blood-pressure, high	: Aakaash-vardhak, Kapha-kaarak, Apaan-vaayu, Vaata-kaarak
Bones, to strengthen	: Prithvi-vardhak
Burning, in the body	: Prithvi-vardhak, Kapha-kaarak, Apaan, Shankha
Blood circulation, slow	: Vyaan, Kapha-shaamak, Pitta-kaarak, Jal-vardhak
Backache	: Vaayu-shaamak, Vaata-naashak, Apaan-vaayu
Bloody stools/urine	: Kapha-kaarak
Burning urination	: Kapha-kaarak, Prithvi vardhak, Apaan, Apaan-vaayu
Blood-pressure, low	: Aakaash-shaamak, Prithvi-vardhak
Bed-wetting	: Jal-shaamak
Boils	: Prithvi-vardhak, Pitta-naashak
Bronchitis	: Prithvi-vardhak
Blocked nose	: Aakaash-shaamak, Prithvi-shaamak, Kapha-naashak
Biliousness	: Prithvi-vardhak, Kapha-kaarak
Brain, to empower	: Vaayu-vardhak, Prithvi-vardhak, Kapha-kaarak

C

Creativity, lack of	: Vaayu-vardhak, Vaata-kaarak, Pitta-kaarak
Cerebral palsy	: Vaayu-vardhak, Vaata-kaarak
Cretinism	: Vaayu-vardhak, Vaata-kaarak
Concentration, lack of	: Vaayu-shaamak, Vaata-naashak
Convulsions	: Vaayu-shaamak, Vaata-naashak
Chorea	: Vaayu-shaamak, Vaata-naashak, Apaan-vaayu
Constipation	: Vaayu-shaamak, Prithvi-shaamak, Jal-vardhak, Vaata-naashak, Apaan, Apaan-vaayu
Congestion, in the body	: Aakaash-vardhak
Chest-congestion	: Aakaash-vardhak
Cartilage, degeneration / tear	: Prithvi-vardhak, Jal-vardhak
Chronic fatigue	: Prithvi-vardhak, Vaata-naashak, Kapha-kaarak, Pushaan
Convalescence	: Prithvi-vardhak
Coldness of body / skin	: Prithvi-shaamak, Jal-shaamak, Vaata-naashak, Pitta-kaarak, Linga
Cervical spondylosis	: Vaayu-shaamak, Prithvi-vardhak, Vaata-naashak, Kapha-kaarak, Apaan, Apaan-vaayu, Jal-vardhak
Cold, intolerance of	: Prithvi-shaamak, Vaata-naashak, Pitta-kaarak, Linga
Cataract	: Prithvi-shaamak
Cracked skin/lips/tongue	: Jal-vardhak, Vaayu-shaamak, Vaata-naashak
Cramps of muscles	: Jal-vardhak, Vaayu-shaamak
Circulation, slow	: Vyaan, Jal-vardhak, Pitta-kaarak, Kapha-shaamak

Chest-pain	: Vaata-naashak, Apaan-vaayu
Colds	: Pitta-kaarak, Kapha-naashak, Linga
Cough, wet	: Pitta-kaarak, Kapha-naashak, Linga
Cough, dry	: Vaayu-shaamak
Colitis	: Kapha-kaarak, Pitta-naashak

D

Dullness of mind	: Vaayu-vardhak, Prithvi-shaamak
Drowsiness	: Vaayu-vardhak, Vaata-kaarak, Prithvi-shaamak
Dementia(s)	: Vaayu-vardhak
Degeneration of retina	: Vaayu-vardhak
Dwarfism	: Vaayu-vardhak
Diabetes mellitus	: Vaayu-vardhak, Kapha-vardhak, Apaan
Dizziness	: Vaayu-shaamak, Prithvi-shaamak
Dry skin/hair	: Vaayu-shaamak, Prithvi-vardhak, Jal-vardhak, Vaata-naashak, Kapha-kaarak, Apaan
Dyspnoea	: Vaayu-shaamak, Asthma
Dysurea	: Prithvi-vardhak, Apaan-vaayu
Detoxification	: Aakaash-vardhak, Apaan
Deafness	: Aakaash-shaamak, Prithvi-vardhak
Debility	: Prithvi-vardhak, Vaata-kaarak, Kapha-kaarak, Apaan
Degeneration of joint-cartilage	: Prithvi-vardhak, Vaayu-shaamak, Jal-vardhak, Apaan, Apaan-vaayu
Dry eyes	: Jal-vardhak
Dehydration	: Jal-vardhak
Deficiency of hormones	: Jal-vardhak
Dropsy	: Jal-shaamak

Diarrhoea	: Jal-shaamak, Vaayu-vardhak, Prithvi-vardhak, Vaata-kaarak, Apaan
Dysentery	: Kapha-kaarak, Apaan
Depression	: Vaayu-vardhak, Prithvi-shaamak
Digestion, weak	: Prithvi-shaamak, Linga, Jal-vardhak, Pitta-kaarak
Duodenal ulcer	: Prithvi-vardhak
Dry mouth/throat	: Jal-vardhak

E

Endocrine disorders	: Vaayu-vardhak/Vaayu-shaamak
Effusion in joints	: Vaayu-vardhak, Jal-shaamak
Epilepsy	: Vaayu-shaamak, Vaata-naashak
E.S.P., to develop	: Aakaash-vardhak
Ear disorders (pain)	: Aakaash-shaamak, Vaata-naashak
(Deafness)	: Aakaash-shaamak, Prithvi-vardhak
Emaciation (weight-loss)	: Prithvi-vardhak, Vaata-naashak, Kapha-kaarak
Excessive salivation/thirst/ perspiration/urination	: Jal-shaamak, Kapha-kaarak
Excessive menses	: Vaata-kaarak, Jal-shaamak, Kapha-kaarak, Prithvi-vardhak
Enthusiasm, lack of	: Vaata-kaarak, Pitta-kaarak, Vaayu-vardhak
Excessive sleep	: Vaata-kaarak, Vaayu-vardhak, Prithvi-shaamak
Eye-ailments, watering	: Pitta-kaarak, Prithvi-shaamak
cataract	: Prithvi-shaamak, Pitta-kaarak
glaucoma	: Jal-shaamak
twitching, nystagmus	; Vaayu-shaamak
Eczema – dry	: Jal-vardhak
– weeping	: Jal-shaamak

F

Frohlick's syndrome : Vaayu-vardhak, Vaata-kaarak
Facial palsy : Vaayu-vardhak
Fear : Vaayu-vardhak, Aakaash-vardhak, Uttarabodhi
Fits : Vaayu-shaamak, Vaata-naashak
Flatulence (gas) : Vaayu-shaamak, Vaata-naashak, Apaan, Apaan-vaayu
Fever : Prithvi-vardhak, Apaan, Shankha
Frozen shoulder : Vaayu-shaamak, Apaan-vaayu
Fatigue : Prithvi-vardhak, Vaata-naashak, Kapha-kaarak, Pushaan
Fracture : Prithvi-vardhak, Kapha-kaarak
Feet, cold : Prithvi-shaamak, Pitta-kaarak, Linga
Fatness : Vaata-kaarak, Prithvi-shaamak, Pitta-kaarak, Linga
Forgetfulness : Vaayu-vardhak, Kapha-kaarak, Prithvi-vardhak
Fissure, anal : Prithvi-vardhak
Frigidity : Prithvi-vardhak, Kapha-kaarak
Flu : Prithvi-vardhak, Apaan, Shankha

G

Gastric ulcer : Prithvi-vardhak
Giddiness : Vaayu-shaamak, vaata-naashak
Gout : Vaayu-shaamak, Apaan-vaayu
Gas : Vaayu-shaamak, Vaata-naashak, Apaan, Apaan-vaayu
General debility : Prithvi-vardhak, Vaata-kaarak, Kapha-kaarak, Apaan
Greying of hair : Prithvi-vardhak, Kapha-kaarak

Greasy skin, hair	:	Vaata-kaarak, Pitta-kaarak
Gall colic	:	Apaan-vaayu
Gastritis	:	Prithvi-vardhak, Kapha-kaarak, Apaan
Glaucoma	:	Jal-shaamak

(H)

Heel-pain	:	Prithvi-shaamak, Apaan-vaayu, Vaata-naashak
Heart, weak / failure	:	Vaayu-vardhak, Vyaan
Heart disease/pain/attack	:	Apaan-vaayu, Aakaash-vardhak, Kapha-kaarak, Vyaan
Hypopituitarism	:	Vaayu-vardhak
Hypothyroidism	:	Vaayu-vardhak, Prithvi-shaamak, Jal-shaamak, Linga, Udaan
Hypoparathyroidism	:	Vaayu-vardhak
Hypoadrenalism	:	Vaayu-vardhak
Hypogonadism	:	Vaayu-vardhak
Hemiplegia	:	Vaayu-vardhak
Hyperthyroidism	:	Vaayu-shaamak, Prithvi-vardhak, Kapha-kaarak
Hiccups	:	Vaayu-shaamak, Apaan-vaayu
High blood pressure	:	Aakaash-vardhak, Kapha-kaarak, Apaan-vaayu, Vaata-kaarak
Hair-loss/greying	:	Prithvi-vardhak, Kapha-kaarak
Hyperacidity	:	Jal-shaamak, Prithvi-vardhak, Kapha-kaarak
Hydrocele	:	Jal-shaamak
Hydrocephalous	:	Jal-shaamak
Hydronephrosis	:	Jal-shaamak
Heat stroke	:	Vaayu-vardhak, Prithvi-vardhak, Shankha
Heat, intolerance	:	Vaata-kaarak, Vaayu-vardhak, Prithvi-vardhak, Kapha-kaarak, Shankha

Headache	: Vaayu-shaamak, Vaata-naashak, Apaan-vaayu
Hoarse voice	: Vaata-naashak, Vaayu-shaamak

I

Initiative, lack of	: Vaayu-vardhak, Vaata-kaarak, Pitta-kaarak
Irritability	: Vaayu-shaamak, Kapha-kaarak
Indecisiveness	: Vaayu-shaamak, Vaata-naashak
Impatience	: Vaayu-shaamak, Vaata-naashak, Prithvi-vardhak, Kapha-kaarak
Intercostal neuralgia	: Vaayu-shaamak
Intuition, to develop	: Aakaash-vardhak
Irregular heart-beats	: Aakaash-vardhak
Inflammatory diseases	: Prithvi-vardhak, Kapha-kaarak
Intolerance of cold	: Prithvi-shaamak, Vaata-naashak, Linga, Pitta-kaarak
Indigestion	: Prithvi-shaamak, Jal-vardhak, Pitta-kaarak, Linga
Intolerance of heat	: Vaayu-vardhak, Vaata-kaarak, Prithvi-vardhak, Kapha-kaarak, Shankha
Irregular menses	: Vaata-naashak, Vaayu-shaamak
Immunity, weak	: Kapha-kaarak, Pushaan
Intelligence, to develop	: Vaayu-vardhak
Impotence	: Prithvi-vardhak, Kapha-kaarak, Linga
Infertility	: Prithvi-vardhak, Jal-vardhak, Kapha-kaarak
Influenza	: Prithvi-vardhak, Apaan, Shankha
Insomnia	: Vaayu-shaamak, Prithvi-vardhak, Vaata-naashak, Kapha-kaarak
Itching	: Prithvi-vardhak, Shankha
Infectious diseases	: Prithvi-vardhak, Kapha-kaarak, Apaan

J

Joint-pains	: Vaayu-shaamak, Vaata-naashak, Prithvi-vardhak, Apaan, Apaan-vaayu, Jal-vardhak, Kapha-kaarak
Jealous nature	: Kapha-kaarak
Jaundice	: Kapha-kaarak
Joy, to induce	: Vaayu-vardhak

K

Kidney ailments	: Apaan, Apaan-vaayu, Jal-shaamak
Kapha (mucous), excessive	: Kapha-naashak mudra

L

Lack of enthusiasm / initiative/creativity	: Vaayu-vardhak, Vaata-kaarak, Pitta-kaarak
Loss of memory	: Vaayu-vardhak, Prithvi-vardhak
Lethargy	: Vaayu-vardhak, Vaata-kaarak
Lack of concentration	: Vaayu-shaamak, Vaata-naashak
Lack of stamina / endurance	: Prithvi-vardhak, Vaata-naashak, Kapha-kaarak
Loss of appetite	: Prithvi-shaamak, Vaata-kaarak, Pitta-kaarak
Loss of taste-sensation	: Jal-vardhak
Loose motions	: Vaata-kaarak, Jal-shaamak, Vaayu-vardhak, Prithvi-vardhak, Apaan
Liver ailments	: Prithvi-shaamak, Linga
Leucorrhoea	: Apaan, Shankha
Lumbago	: Vaayu-shaamak, Vaata-naashak, Apaan-vaayu
Laryngitis	: Prithvi-vardhak
Leprosy	: Kapha-kaarak

Ⓜ

Mind, to empower : Vaayu-vardhak
Muscles, to strengthen : Vaayu-vardhak, Shankha
Memory, loss of : Vaayu-vardhak, Prithvi-vardhak, Kapha-kaarak
Mental retardation : Vaayu-vardhak
Multiple sclerosis : Vaayu-vardhak
Motor neuron disease : Vaayu-vardhak
Myxoedema : Vaayu-vardhak, Jal-shaamak, Prithvi-shaamak, Linga
Myopathies : Vaayu-vardhak, Prithvi-vardhak
Myesthenia gravis : Vaayu-vardhak
Monoplegia : Vaayu-vardhak
Mucous, excessive : Vaayu-vardhak, Pitta-kaarak, Linga
Muscle spasm/cramps/rigidity : Vaayu-shaamak, Jal-vardhak
Milk, deficient : Jal-vardhak
Migraine : Aakaash-vardhak, Vaayu-vardhak, Apaan
Muscle-atrophy : Prithvi-vardhak
Mouth ulcers : Prithvi-vardhak, Kapha-kaarak
Menstrual problems:
Scanty : Jal-vardhak, Vaata-naashak, Prithvi-shaamak
Excessive : Jal-shaamak, Vaata-kaarak, Prithvi-vardhak, Kapha-kaarak
Painful : Vaata-naashak, Kapha-kaarak, Apaan-vaayu
Irregular : Vaata-naashak, Vaayu-shaamak
Mental tension : Kapha-kaarak
Menopause : Jal-vardhak, Kapha-kaarak

N

Nervous (system) disorders : Vaayu-vardhak, Vaata-kaarak
Neuritis : Vaayu-vardhak, Prithvi-vardhak
Neuropathies : Vaayu-vardhak
Nystagmus : Vaayu-shaamak
Numbness in body / hands / feet : Vaayu-shaamak, Aakaash-shaamak, Vaata-naashak
Nose/smell disorders : Prithvi-vardhak
Nose, running : Jal-shaamak
Nose, blocked : Prithvi-shaamak, Kapha-naashak
Nervous exhaustion / breakdown : Vaata-kaarak, Vaayu-vardhak
Neck-pain, stiffness : Vaayu-shaamak, Apaan-vaayu
Nails, brittle : Vaayu-shaamak, Vaata-naashak, Prithvi-vardhak
Nausea : Apaan, Apaan-vaayu, Vaayu-shaamak

O

Optic atrophy : Vaayu-vardhak, Prithvi-vardhak
Overactivity of endocrine glands : Vaayu-shaamak
Osteoporosis/osteomalacia : Prithvi-vardhak
Osteo-Arthritis (O.A.) : Vaayu-shaamak, Prithvi-vardhak, Vaata-naashak, Kapha-kaarak, Apaan, Apaan-vaayu, Jal-vardhak
Obesity : Prithvi-shaamak, Vaata-kaarak, Pitta-kaarak, Linga, Vaayu-vardhak
Oliguria : Jal-vardhak, Vaata-naashak
Oligomenorrhoea : Jal-vardhak, Pitta-kaarak
Oligospermia : Jal-vardhak

Oedema	: Jal-shaamak, Prithvi-shaamak, Linga
Oily skin/hair	: Pitta-kaarak, Vaayu-vardhak, Vaata-kaarak

P

Paresis, Polio, Paralysis, paraplegia	: Vaayu-vardhak, Prithvi-vardhak, Kapha-kaarak
Paralytic squint	: Vaayu-vardhak
Ptosis	: Vaayu-vardhak
Prostatitis	: Prithvi-vardhak, Kapha-kaarak
Parkinson's disease	: Vaayu-shaamak, Vaata-naashak, Apaan-vaayu
Palpitations	: Vaayu-shaamak, Apaan-vaayu
Premature ageing/ greying of hair	: Prithvi-vardhak, Kapha-kaarak
Psoriasis	: Vaayu-shaamak, Jal-vardhak
Pleurisy/Pleural effusion	: Jal-shaamak
Painful conditions	: Vaayu-shaamak, Vaata-naashak, Apaan-vaayu
Piles	: Apaan, Apaan-vaayu, Prithvi-vardhak
Pharyngitis (sore throat)	: Prithvi-vardhak, Kapha-kaarak, Shankha
Pneumonia	: Prithvi-vardhak, Kapha-kaarak, Shankha
Pituitary/Pineal disorders	: Vaayu-vardhak
Pitta (Bile), excessive	: Pitta-naashak mudra

Q

Quadriplegia	: Vaayu-vardhak, Prithvi-vardhak, Kapha-kaarak

R

Respiratory paralysis	: Vaayu-vardhak, Udaan
Restlessness	: Vaayu-shaamak
Rigidity, of muscles	: Vaayu-shaamak
Running nose	: Jal-shaamak
Rheumatoid Arthritis	: Vaayu-shaamak, Prithvi-vardhak, Kapha-kaarak, Apaan-vaayu
Renal colic	: Apaan-vaayu
Retinal degeneration	: Vaayu-vardhak

S

Syringomyelia	: Vaayu-vardhak
Simmond's disease	: Vaayu-vardhak
Spasticity of muscles	: Vaayu-shaamak, Jal-vardhak
Stress	: Vaayu-shaamak, Vaata-naashak
Sleeplessness	: Vaayu-shaamak, Prithvi-vardhak, Vaata-naashak, Kapha-kaarak
Sciatica	: Vaayu-shaamak
Skin, dry-cracked	: Vaayu-shaamak, Prithvi-vardhak, Jal-vardhak, Kapha-kaarak, Vaata-naashak, Apaan
Mature, ageing	: Prithvi-vardhak
Oily	: Vaata-kaarak, Vaayu-vardhak, Pitta-kaarak
Cold	: Prithvi-shaamak, Vaata-naashak, Pitta-kaarak, Linga
Sinusitis	: Aakaash-vardhak, Prithvi-vardhak, Shankha
Skin rashes	: Prithvi-vardhak, Kapha-kaarak
Stomach, burning in	: Prithvi-vardhak, Kapha-kaarak, Apaan, Shankha
Stomach, pain	: Vaayu-shaamak, Vaata-naashak, Apaan-vaayu

Shivering : Prithvi-shaamak, Vaata-naashak, Linga
Sweating, absent : Prithvi-shaamak, Vaata-naashak, Pitta-kaarak
Sweating, excessive : Vaata-kaarak, Jal-shaamak, Prithvi-vardhak
Scanty, urine : Jal-vardhak, Vaata-naashak, Kapha-kaarak
Scanty menses : Jal-vardhak, Pitta-kaarak, Vaata-naashak, Prithvi-shaamak
Scanty semen : Jal-vardhak
Saliva, excessive : Jal-shaamak, Kapha-kaarak
Sleep, excessive : Vaayu-vardhak, Vaata-kaarak, Prithvi-shaamak
Sun-stroke : Vaata-kaarak, Prithvi-vardhak, Shankha
Stamina, lack of : Vaayu-vardhak, Prithvi-vardhak, Kapha-kaarak, Apaan, Pushaan
Stammering : Vaayu-shaamak, Vaata-naashak, Shankha
Sexual debility : Linga, Prithvi-vardhak, Kapha-kaarak
Shoulder pain / stiffness : Apaan-vaayu
Swelling : Prithvi-shaamak, Jal-shaamak
Sore throat : Prithvi-vardhak, Kapha-kaarak, Shankha

T

Tabes dorsalis : Vaayu-vardhak
Tongue/taste disorders : Jal-vardhak
Thyroid, underactive : Udaan, Vaayu-vardhak, Prithvi-shaamak, Jal-shaamak, Pitta-kaarak, Linga
Typhoid : Prithvi-vardhak, Shankha

T.B.	: Prithvi-vardhak
Tennis elbow	: Vaayu-shaamak, Apaan-vaayu
Thyroid, overactive	: Vaayu-shaamak, Prithvi-vardhak, Kapha-kaarak
Timidity	: Vaayu-shaamak, Vaata-naashak, Prithvi-vardhak
Tremors	: Vaayu-shaamak, Vaata-naashak, Apaan-vaayu
Throat-burning/pain	: Prithvi-vardhak, Apaan-vaayu, Shankha
Toothache	: Apaan-vaayu, Vaata-naashak
Tonsillitis	: Prithvi-vardhak, Apaan
Trigeminal neuralgia	: Vaayu-shaamak, Apaan-vaayu
Tinnitus (noises in the ear)	: Aakaash-shaamak
Tachycardia (fast heart-beats)	: Vaayu-shaamak

(U)

Urticaria, itching	: Prithvi-vardhak, Kapha-kaarak, Shankha
Ulcers, in mouth / stomach / intestines	: Prithvi-vardhak, Kapha-kaarak
Urine, scanty / absent	: Vaayu-shaamak, Vaata-naashak, jal-vardhak, Apaan
Profuse / Frequent	: Vaata-kaarak, Vaayu-vardhak, Jal-shaamak
Burning / painful	: Prithvi-vardhak, Apaan, Apaan-vaayu
Unsteady walk (gait)	: Vaayu-shaamak, Vaata-naashak
Ulcerative colitis	: Prithvi-vardhak, Kapha-kaarak, Pitta-naashak

(V)

Vocal paralysis : Vaayu-vardhak
Voice, lost / feeble : Vaayu-vardhak
Voice, hoarse / strained : Vaayu-shaamak, Prithvi-vardhak
Vertigo : Vaayu-shaamak, Vaata-naashak
Vision problems : Prithvi-shaamak
Vaata (air), excessive : Vaata-naashak mudra
Varicose veins : Apaan, Apaan-vaayu, Prithvi-vardhak

(W)

Weakness : Vaayu-vardhak, Vaata-kaarak, Prithvi-vardhak, Kapha-kaarak, Apaan
Weight-loss (to arrest) : Prithvi-vardhak, Vaayu-shaamak, Vaata-naashak
Weight, excessive : prithvi-shaamak, Vaayu-vardhak, Pitta-kaarak, Linga
Water retention : Jal-shaamak, Prithvi-shaamak, Linga
Watery eyes : Jal-shaamak, Pitta-kaarak

6. APPENDIX : DIETARY SUGGESTIONS

Vaata constitution

People with an excess of Vaata humor in their bodies should, in general, restrict foods with pungent, bitter or astringent tastes. They should also keep away from cold foods, stale foods and dry snacks.

The following foods can further aggravate Vaata humor and should be curtailed :

(1) All pulses (legumes)

(2) Cereals (grains) : Barley, corn, millets (bajra), oats (jowar), rye.

(3) Vegetables : Green leafy vegetables, brinjals (egg plant), cabbage, cauliflower, cucumber, french beans (phansi), gawaar (cluster beans), (raw) onions, (green) peas, potatoes, sweet gourd (dudhi or louki), tomatoes, turai (ridge gourd).

(4) Fruits : All dry fruits, pear, pomegranate, water-melon.

(5) Betel-nuts (supari)

The following foods pacify Vaata humor and are, therefore, beneficial :

(1) Cereals (grains) : Wheat, rice.

(2) Pulses (legumes) : (in small quantities) Moong, urad.

(3) Vegetables (all cooked) : Beet, carrots, onions (cooked), pumpkin, raddish, sweet potatoes, tomatoes (ripe).

(4) Fruits : Apple, aavla (goose berry), banana, bor (ber), cherries, figs (fresh), grapes, guava (peru, amrood), mango, melons, papaya, peach, pineapple, plum, sweet lime (mosambi).

(5) All nuts, oils and dairy products (esp. butter milk) allowed.

(6) Fennel seeds (saunf, variyaali) and betel leaves allowed.

Pitta constitution

People with an excess of Pitta humor in their bodies should, in general, restrict the intake of foods with pungent, sour or salty tastes. They should also keep away from stimulants like tea, coffee, tobacco, cola drinks, alcohol, etc. Spicy foods should also be avoided.

The following foods can futher aggravate Pitta humor and should be curtailed :

(1) Pulses (legumes) : Chola, urad.

(2) Cereals (grains) : Corn, millets (bajra), brown rice, rye.

(3) Vegetables : Beet, brinjals (egg plant), carrots, garlic, karela (bitter gourd), onions, raddish, tomatoes.

(4) Fruits : All sour fruits, banana, berries, cherries, green grapes, lemon, orange, papaya, peach, pineapple, plum.

(5) Nuts : avoid all except coconut.

(6) Dairy products : Buttermilk, curds, cheese.

(7) Oils : Corn, sunflower, til (sesame).

(8) Honey

The following foods pacify Pitta humor and are, therefore, beneficial :

(1) Pulses (legumes) : Chana (gram), green peas, math (matki), moong, masoor (red lentils), soyabeans, tur, vaal.

(2) Cereals (grains) : Barley, basmati rice, oats (jowar), wheat.

(3) Vegetables : Cabbage, cauliflower, cucumber, french beans (phansi), gawaar (cluster beans), green leafy vegetables, green peas, potatoes, pumpkin, turai (ridge gourd), sweet gourd (dudhi or louki).

(4) Fruits : All sweet fruits, aavla (goose berry), apple, apricots, ber (bor), black grapes, chickoo, coconut, dates, figs, guava (peru or amrood), jack fruit (phanas), jamoon, mango, melons, pear, pomegranate, seetafal (custard apple).

(5) Dairy products : Milk, butter, ghee, ice cream.

(6) Oils : Coconut, soya, sunflower.

(7) Betel-nuts (supari)

Kapha constitution

People with an excess Kapha humor in their bodies should, in general, restrict the intake of foods with sweet, sour or salty tastes.

The following foods can further aggravate Kapha humor and should be curtailed :

(1) **Pulses (legumes) :** Moong, soyabeans, urad, chola.

(2) **Cereals (grains) :** Millets (bajra), oats (jowar), (new) rice, wheat.

(3) **Vegetables :** Cucumber, french beans (phansi), gawaar (cluster beans), pumpkin, sweet gourd (dudhi or louki), sweet potatoes, tomatoes, turai (ridge gourd).

(4) **Fruits :** Bananas, coconuts, fresh figs, grapes, guava (peru or amrood), lemon, melons, oranges, papaya, pineapple, plums.

(5) **Dairy products :** Avoid all except ghee.

(6) **Oils :** Avoid all except (small quantities of) corn, sunflower.

(7) **Nuts**

The following foods can pacify Kapha and are, therefore, beneficial :

(1) **Pulses (legumes) :** Chana (gram), green peas, math (matki), masoor (red lentils), tur, vaal.

(2) **Cereals (grains) :** Barley, corn, basmati rice.

(3) **Vegetables :** Beet, brinjals (egg plant), cabbage, carrots, cauliflower, cucumber, garlic, green leafy vegetables, green peas, karela (bitter gourd), lady's fingers (okra), onions, potatoes, raddish, tomatoes.

(4) **Fruits :** Aavla (goose berry), apple, berries, cherries, figs (dry), jamoon, mango, peach, pear, pomegranate.

(5) **Oils :** Small quantities of corn and/or sunflower oils.

(6) **Dairy products :** Small quantity of ghee.

(7) Betel-leaves, betel nuts, fennel seeds (saunf or variyali).

SC

Printed by Ambica Mudranalay,